Curry Easy

Curry Easy
Madhur Jaffrey

EBURY
PRESS

for Sanford

11

Ebury Press, an imprint of Ebury Publishing,
20 Vauxhall Bridge Road,
London SW1V 2SA

Ebury Publishing is part of the Penguin Random House
group of companies whose addresses can be found at
global.penguinrandomhouse.com

 Penguin
Random House
UK

Text copyright © Madhur Jaffrey 2010

Photography copyright © Ebury Press 2010, except
for pages 10, 44, 70, 106, 138, 176, 198, 223, 228,
258 © Jean Cazals 2010
Photographs on pages 6 and 204 by Christopher Hirsheimer

Madhur Jaffrey has asserted her right to be identified as the
author of this Work in accordance with the Copyright,
Designs and Patents Act 1988

First published by Ebury Press in 2010
www.penguin.co.uk

A CIP catalogue record for this book is available from the
British Library

Design: 'OME DESIGN
Photography: Jean Cazals
Food styling: Marie-Ange Lapierre
Prop styling: Penny Markham

ISBN 9780091923143

Printed and bound in China by C& C Offset Printing
Co. Limited

Penguin Random House is committed to a sustainable
future for our business, our readers and our planet. This book
is made from Forest Stewardship Council® certified paper.

 MIX
Paper from
responsible sources
FSC® C018179

Contents

Introduction

The techniques used in Indian cookery are not any different from those used the world over: roasting, grilling, steaming, frying, stewing, braising. What gives Indian cuisine its uniqueness, its tingling excitement and its health-giving properties, is the knowledgeable use of spices and seasonings, which is ancient in its provenance. It is this very use of spices and seasonings that appears daunting to many approaching Indian cooking for the first time.

My purpose in writing this book is to vanquish that fear, to make Indian dishes as simple and straightforward to prepare as, say, a beef stew, to hold your hand through the entire process with clear instructions and detailed explanations.

My own cooking has changed over the years. I am often as rushed for time as perhaps you are. I am always asking myself, is there an easier way to do this? So, over these decades, I have simplified my cooking greatly. I now try to reach real Indian tastes by using simpler methods and fewer steps. It is these newer recipes that you will find in this book. Just to give you an example: to make a proper curry called for the browning of wet seasonings, such as onion, garlic and ginger, the browning of dry spices, such as cumin, chillies and coriander, and the browning of the meat itself. Now I find that if I just marinate the meat with all the spices and seasonings and then bake it, both covered and uncovered, all the browning happens on its own, the curry absorbs the spices and is delicious.

I also searched for recipes that are simple to begin with. India has so many of those. Very often all you require is a little oil, a few whole spices and then the vegetable or fish. Sauté and it is done. No fuss at all. Prawns, potatoes, peas... they can all be cooked this way.

I have also used a smaller palette of spices. There is still a good range of them because Indian food would not be as magical without them. But these days going out to look for spices and seasonings is no longer necessary as all of them are available online around the world. Yes, your fingers can do the walking! And if you are adding one spice at a certain stage of the cooking, you can just as easily add three or four or six.

Read the recipes thoroughly before starting to cook as sometimes an overnight marination is required. Also, it is a good idea to have all the preparations done and the spices measured out beforehand as seasonings might need to go into the cooking pot in quick succession. For spices that need to be ground, I use a coffee-grinder set aside for them, but a mortar and pestle will do.

The recipes in this book come mainly from India, but include the whole family of South Asian nations. What you will therefore discover within these pages

are dishes such as mouth-watering Okra Sambol with slivers of shallots and tomatoes (page 233) and crispy Fried Whitebait (page 28), perfect with drinks, from Sri Lanka; a warming Spinach and Ginger Soup Perfumed with Cloves (page 42) and a creamy coconut Goan Prawn Curry from India (page 64); meaty Grilled Lamb Chops (page 118) and Bhuna Quail from Pakistan (page 105); and a soulful White Chicken Korma (page 93) and a perky Sweet and Sour Butternut Squash or Pumpkin from Bangladesh (page 170). I love them all and you can make them with ease.

For most Indians, the centre of the meal is the starch, usually rice or bread, or in some cases both. Then there are all the things you eat with it. There is meat or fish (at banquets both may be served), one or two vegetables, some kind of dal (dried beans or split peas), some form of yoghurt, a salad and a selection of pickles and chutneys. Vegetarians would, of course, leave out the meat or fish. I have offered serving suggestions with some of the main dishes, but feel free to make your own choice. I have not always added the dals and relishes to these suggestions, but remember, they are the constants, present at most full meals. I have used the word dal frequently in this book. Even though dal is, technically, a dried split pea, the term is commonly used for all legumes – dried beans *and* split peas. When Indians talk

about having dined, they say, 'I have eaten my *dal bhat* (dal and rice) or *dal roti* (dal and bread).' Dal is a very important part of the meal.

You may also serve some of the dishes in this book with Western accompaniments, or use these dishes as accompaniments to Western foods. For example, Minced Turkey with Hyderabadi Seasonings (see page 102) may be served with hot corn tortillas and a salsa, and Pakistani-style Grilled Lamb Chops (see page 118) may be served with boiled potatoes and sautéed spinach. Do what is easy and comfortable.

Pick out any dish in this book you wish to cook. Buy the spices for just one recipe. Don't overwhelm yourself – you will find the process will be much easier than you thought and the results quite delicious.

Starters, Snacks & Soups

Indians do not really eat starters. In most homes an announcement is made that lunch or dinner is ready. Everyone goes first to wash their hands and then to take their place at the table – or on the floor, if that is where the food is to be consumed. Most of the food appears at the same time – the meats, the vegetables, the rice or breads, the legumes, the yoghurt relishes, the salads, pickles and chutneys. At the end of the meal there is fresh fruit. There are some Indian communities, however, that do eat their meals in courses. The Bohra Muslims of Gujarat, for example, have banquets at which they alternate between salty and sweet dishes, and actually start with a pinch of salt; the Bengalis of east India and the Tamils of the south are known to have each of their courses with rice; at festive dinners Bengalis might start with rice and a crisp fritter, whereas a Tamil might begin his everyday meal with rice, some ghee (clarified butter) and a prayer.

When Indian restaurants began opening up around the world in the 1950s they were modelled on Western ones, and it was thought that some form of first course was needed. So the restaurateurs dug into India's vast repertoire of snack foods, colonial soups, the world of kebabs and tandoori meats and came up with… starters. Housewives entertaining at home, the one writing this book included, have continued along the same path, adapting whatever we possibly could to fit into this new, Western category of food.

Some of the dishes in this chapter may be served with drinks – the poppadoms, spicy popcorn, nuts, fried whitebait and kebabs. The cheese toast may be served with tea. The mushrooms and aubergine dishes are first courses, as are all the soups.

Is it a part of India's culinary tradition to offer soups? Yes and no. Well, that is India for you. You can never get a simple answer. In India's Muslim culinary tradition there is *aab gosht* (meat broth), which is served at the start of a meal. Then, during our colonial period, the British introduced us to so many soups that we began to suspect that these watery concoctions were what sustained the Empire. Of course, when Indians made soups in their homes, they were Indianised – with some ginger here, some cloves and green chillies there. Then there is a third category – India's ancient soupy dishes that are served as part of the main meal, but are quite amenable to being served as a first course. There is *rasam*, the 'pepper water' of Tamil Nadu, from which the British concocted mulligatawny; the *saars* of Maharashtra, which are often spiced fruit purées; and the various types of *kadhi* from northern and western India, which have beaten yoghurt thickened with *gram* (chickpea) flour as their base. And who can forget the magnificent *dal dhokli* of Gujarat, a spicy mix of split peas and tomatoes with some pappardelle-type home-made pasta ribbons floating around in it.

Poppadoms

Known by different names in the north and south of India, these crisp wafers are an essential part of Indian cuisine, as 'something with a crunch' completes a meal in many parts of India. Known as *papadums* in the south and *papar* or *papad* in the north, they are generally made out of a split-pea dough that is rolled out into paper-thin discs and dried in the sun (the desert areas of India are ideal for this). The ones I like best are made of urad dal and flavoured with peppercorns. You buy them from Indian grocers, but they still need cooking. The traditional way is to fry them in very hot oil for a few seconds, which makes them expand into marvellous architectural shapes à la Frank Gehry. Now I just do them in the microwave oven. They do not expand as much, but they can still take on Zaha Hadid-style shapes and are wonderfully crunchy without being oily. Make as many poppadoms as you wish, and serve them with drinks or as part of the meal **Makes 1**

1 poppadom

Break the poppadom in half. Put a piece of kitchen paper into the microwave oven and place the poppadom halves on top, with straight edges facing outwards. Microwave on full power for 40–60 seconds, depending upon the strength of your oven.

Seasoned Radishes

I love these radishes and cannot stop eating them. I like to offer them with drinks, but you may serve them with grilled meats or as a relish with a meal   **Serves 4**

12 medium radishes

½ teaspoon salt

¼ teaspoon cayenne pepper

1 tablespoon red wine vinegar

Remove the radish tops and tails. Wash the radishes well, then cut them in half lengthways. Combine with all the other ingredients in a small bowl, mix well and set aside for 3 hours, tossing every now and then. Drain the radishes and serve.

Spiced Roasted Cashews

When I was growing up in Delhi, my mother regularly deep-fried cashews for us in a *karhai*, an Indian wok (many anthropologists believe that the utensil actually originated in India). She would scoop them up from the hot oil with a slotted spoon and leave them to drain on a crisp sheet of brown paper, the same type she used to cover our school books. My father ate the nuts with his evening whisky and soda, and the rest of us nibbled on them with our soft drinks. I have now taken to roasting the cashews instead. Nothing could be easier   **Serves 6–8 with drinks**

150 g/5½ oz raw cashew nuts

1 teaspoon olive or
  rapeseed oil

½ teaspoon salt

½ teaspoon ground cumin
  seeds

½ teaspoon cayenne pepper

Preheat the oven to 180°C/gas mark 4.

Line a small baking tin with foil and spread the cashews out in a single layer. Dribble the oil over them and toss well so that the oil clings to them like a film. Sprinkle the salt, cumin and cayenne pepper over them and toss thoroughly again. Place in the centre of the oven and bake for 12–15 minutes, tossing and mixing every 4–5 minutes. Leave to cool and firm up before serving.

Roasted Almonds with Black Pepper

Black pepper is native to India. Long before India had red chillies to make foods hot, it relied on black pepper. This recipe harks back to a period that is still part of India's present **Serves 6–8 with drinks**

150 g/5½ oz whole, blanched almonds

1 teaspoon olive or rapeseed oil

½ teaspoon salt

½ teaspoon ground cumin seeds

about ½ teaspoon freshly ground black pepper

Preheat the oven to 180°C/gas mark 4.

Line a small baking tin with foil and spread the almonds out in a single layer. Dribble the oil over them and toss well so that the oil clings to them like a film. Sprinkle the salt, cumin and black pepper over them, and toss thoroughly again. Place in the centre of the oven and bake for 12–15 minutes, tossing and mixing every 4–5 minutes. Leave to cool and firm up before serving.

Perfumed Almonds

Almonds are considered 'brain food' in India. They were always given to us in the morning, especially before exams, after they had been soaked overnight and then peeled. Each one of us got seven almonds. Don't ask me why. So here is a delicious, lightly perfumed morning dose for two people. The soaking makes them taste a bit like green almonds. The perfume is an added bonus. You may serve them with drinks. I often offer dinner guests a few of these almonds just before I serve dessert and coffee **Serves 2**

14 whole almonds with skin

5 cardamom pods

1 tablespoon caster sugar

Put the almonds, cardamom pods and sugar in a small bowl. Pour 250 ml/8 fl oz of boiling water over the top, stir and leave to soak for 12 hours. Refrigerate if leaving longer.

Remove from the water, peel and serve.

Spicy Popcorn

You can make this with ready-made popcorn (you will need about 4.5 litres/8¾ pints-worth – use a measuring jug), but it is more fun to pop the corn and season it yourself. If you have your own method of popping corn, do use it. My method is below **Makes enough to fill a 4.5-litre/8¾-pint bowl**

5 tablespoons olive or rapeseed oil

200 g/7 oz popping corn

¹⁄₁₆ teaspoon ground asafoetida (optional)

1½ teaspoons brown mustard seeds

3 tablespoons beige sesame seeds

½ teaspoon ground turmeric

2 teaspoons salt

2 teaspoons caster sugar

½ teaspoon cayenne pepper

⅙ teaspoon ground cloves

¹⁄₁₆ teaspoon ground cinnamon

To pop the corn, put 3 tablespoons of the oil in a large pan and set on medium–high heat. When hot, put in just a small fistful of the measured popcorn and cover with a lid. You will hear the corn popping. Let it continue for a few seconds. When most of it is done, move the pot to the side and leave covered for exactly 30 seconds (you can count).

Put the pan back on the heat and add all the remaining popcorn. Cover and shake. After 3 seconds, turn the heat down to medium. Shake the pan as the corn pops. When all the popping is done, turn off the heat.

Put the remaining 2 tablespoons of oil in a small frying pan and set on a medium–high heat. When hot, put in the asafoetida, then the mustard seeds, then the sesame seeds. As soon as the seeds start to pop, a matter of seconds, take the pan off the heat and add the turmeric. Stir well.

Empty the contents of the pan over the popcorn. Add the remaining ingredients and toss thoroughly.

Chickpeas for Nibbling

There is nothing like sitting down for an evening drink with these chickpeas by one's side. I like to use organic canned chickpeas, but any will do. If you have access to an Indian grocer, do sprinkle the chickpeas with some chaat masala (see page 261) at the end. It gives them an extra spiciness, but is not essential. These are best eaten the day they are made **Serves 4 with drinks**

1 x 400-g/14-oz can chickpeas

1 teaspoon ground cumin seeds

1 teaspoon ground coriander seeds

¼ teaspoon cayenne pepper

½–¾ teaspoon salt

1 tablespoon chickpea flour, or plain white flour

1½ tablespoons olive or rapeseed oil, plus more for greasing

¼ teaspoon chaat masala (optional)

Preheat the oven to 200°C/gas mark 6.

Drain the chickpeas, then dry them thoroughly with several changes of kitchen paper. Put them in a bowl. Add the cumin, coriander, cayenne pepper and salt. Toss to mix. Add the flour and toss again. Add the oil and mix well.

Grease a small baking tin (18 x 25 cm/7 x 10 inches is ideal) and empty the chickpeas into it, spreading them out evenly. Bake for 15 minutes. Stir the chickpeas around and bake for another 10–15 minutes. Remove from the oven.

Sprinkle the chaat masala over the top, if using, and toss. Serve immediately if you wish.

Cheese Toast

I love cheese toast the way it is done in India – with some chopped fresh green chillies and fresh coriander thrown in. We like to serve it with tea as we seem to love the combination of spicy snacks and very hot tea. You can use any white bread (or brown, if you prefer), any cheese (I happen to like sharp Cheddar), and the chillies could be fresh (¼ teaspoon, well chopped), but the pickled Greek ones are fine too. As I always have the latter on hand in my refrigerator and I like the tartness they provide, I use them instead. Some Anglo–Indian recipes have the yolks of hard-boiled eggs mixed with mustard spread under the cheese as well. I make my toast in a frying pan, but use a panini press or toasted sandwich maker, if you have one. **Serves 1**

2 thin slices of cheese (sized to fit the bread)

2 slices of bread

5–6 rings of pickled hot Greek peppers, drained and patted dry

1 teaspoon very finely chopped fresh coriander

1 tablespoon melted butter or olive oil

Put 1 slice of cheese on 1 slice of bread, making sure to cover it completely. Spread the pepper rings evenly on top. Sprinkle the fresh coriander over that. Cover with the second slice of cheese and the second slice of bread and press down.

Brush a small, heavy-based frying pan with half the butter and set over a medium–high heat. When hot, place the sandwich in it, pressing down. Cook until golden brown, pressing down frequently with a spatula. Meanwhile, brush the top of the sandwich with the remaining butter. Flip it over and brown the second side, pressing down again.

To serve, cut it in half, if you like, and eat immediately.

Stir-fried Peas in Their Pods

Here is a dish that, as far as I know, was served in India only by my own family. It was made only when peas were young and fresh. Even Indians who dine with us in the pea season are surprised by it. I grow my own peas and this is the first dish I make with them when they are ready for picking. You have to eat the peas rather like artichoke leaves: put the whole pea pod in your mouth, hold on to it by its stem end, then clench your teeth and pull. What you get to eat are not just the peas themselves but also the softened pods. You discard the fibrous bits after getting all the goodness out of them. We ate this as a snack or at teatime, but I have taken to serving it as a first course **Serves 4**

2 tablespoons olive or
  rapeseed oil

⅛ teaspoon ground asafoetida

½ teaspoon whole cumin seeds

560 g/1¼ lb fresh whole peas
  in their pods, washed but
  with stems still attached

¼ teaspoon salt

¼ teaspoon cayenne pepper

1 teaspoon lemon juice

Put the oil in a *karhai*, wok or large sauté pan and set over a medium–high heat. When hot, add the asafoetida and cumin seeds. Let the seeds sizzle for 5 seconds, then add the peas, salt and cayenne pepper. Stir for a minute and add 4 tablespoons water. Cover, lower the heat and cook for about 10 minutes, or until the peas are cooked through.

Add the lemon juice and stir until all the liquid has been absorbed. Serve hot or at room temperature.

Stir-fried Spicy Mushrooms

I often serve these as a starter. I offer them just the way they are, but you could also serve them on toasted slices of Italian bread or ordinary buttered toast **Serves 4**

5 tablespoons olive oil

½ teaspoon whole brown mustard seeds

¼ teaspoon whole fennel seeds

15 fresh curry leaves or 10 fresh basil leaves, torn

450 g/1 lb cremini or plain white, medium-sized mushrooms, cut lengthways into slices 5 mm/¼ inch thick

1 clove garlic, peeled and sliced

salt

⅛ teaspoon cayenne pepper

2–3 teaspoons lime or lemon juice

1–2 tablespoons finely chopped fresh coriander or parsley

Put the oil in a large frying pan and set over a medium–high heat. When hot, drop in the mustard seeds. As soon as they start to pop, a matter of seconds, add the fennel seeds and curry leaves. A few seconds later, add the mushrooms and garlic. Stir and fry until the liquid begins to ooze out of the mushrooms, about 2 minutes. Now add about ⅓–½ teaspoon salt (taste as you go), some cayenne pepper and lime juice. Stir for a minute.

Taste for balance of seasonings. Add the coriander, stir, and turn off the heat. Serve warm or at room temperature.

Grilled Aubergine Slices with Yoghurt Sauce

Here you simply marinate aubergine slices in a spicy dressing and then grill them. When serving (hot or cold), spoon a dollop of yoghurt seasoned with fresh mint on the top. It is cool and refreshing **Serves 4–6**

For the marinade

2 tablespoons red wine vinegar

1 tablespoon Dijon mustard

1½ tablespoons caster sugar

1½ teaspoons salt

2 tablespoons Tabasco sauce

2 tablespoons peeled and finely chopped fresh ginger

1 tablespoon ground cumin

1 tablespoon peeled and finely chopped garlic

4 tablespoons tomato juice (canned will do) or chopped tomatoes

4 tablespoons chopped fresh coriander

2 tablespoons olive or rapeseed oil

To prepare the aubergines

1 large aubergine, weighing about 560 g/1¼ lb

⅛ teaspoon salt

⅛ teaspoon cayenne pepper

4–5 leaves fresh mint, finely chopped

120 ml/4 fl oz natural yoghurt

Put all the ingredients for the marinade into a blender and blend until smooth. Pour into a large bowl.

Cut the aubergine crossways into round slices about 1 cm/½ inch thick, and add to the bowl of marinade. Toss to coat, then cover and refrigerate for 6–8 hours or overnight, turning the slices a few times whenever convenient.

Heat the grill to its highest setting. Lift the aubergine slices out of the marinade and lay them in a single layer in the bottom of a grill pan. Grill 10–13 cm/4–5 inches from the heat for 7–8 minutes a side, moving the slices around so that they brown evenly.

Add the salt, cayenne pepper and mint to the yoghurt and mix well.

When serving the aubergine, put a dollop of the yoghurt mixture on top of each slice.

Aubergine with Fennel & Cumin

Indians do not eat starters as such (soups being perhaps the only exception), but there are many Indian dishes that can be served as a first course. This aubergine dish is one of them. I often serve it as such, with a slice of French bread on the side and some Pinot Grigio to polish it off. You can, of course, also serve it as the vegetable dish with the main course. (I love it with the Tandoori-style Duck Breasts on page 103.)

Serves 4–6

1 medium aubergine, weighing about 450 g/1 lb

6 tablespoons olive or corn oil

1 medium onion, cut into half-rings about 5 mm/¼ inch thick

½ teaspoon whole cumin seeds

½ teaspoon whole fennel seeds

120 ml/4 fl oz tomato passata (see page 268)

1 teaspoon salt

1 teaspoon granulated sugar

¼ teaspoon cayenne pepper

300 ml/10 fl oz water

Cut the aubergine lengthways into 3 slabs. Now cut the slabs into chunky chips about 5 cm/2 inches long and 3 cm/1¼ inches wide and thick.

Pour the oil into a large frying pan or sauté pan and set over a medium–high heat. When hot, add the onion, the cumin and fennel seeds and the aubergine. Fry, stirring, for about 5 minutes, or until the onion just starts to brown. Add the passata, salt, sugar, cayenne pepper and water. Bring to the boil. Cover, lower the heat and simmer gently, turning the aubergine pieces now and then, until they are really tender, about 30–35 minutes.

Baked Pâté Kebabs

Before cooking, the meat–spice mixture requires a rest in the refrigerator to bring all the flavours together and to give the kebabs their requisite melt-in-the-mouth tenderness. If you cannot get a loaf tin of the size specified, something a bit smaller or larger will do. (You could also use a 15-cm/6-inch square cake tin and cut the kebabs into rectangles, in which case, bake for only 30 minutes.) Serve these pâté-like kebabs with drinks, offering flatbread pieces or savoury biscuits to eat them with, or serve them as part of a meal with vegetables or salads. They need an accompaniment, such as the Peshawari Red Pepper Chutney or the Bengali-style Tomato Chutney (see page 238 or 239) **Serves 8 as a starter, 4 as a main course**

450 g/1 lb minced turkey, preferably equal amounts of dark and light meat

2 tablespoons finely chopped fresh mint

2 tablespoons finely chopped fresh coriander

2–3 cloves garlic, peeled and crushed

¾–1 teaspoon cayenne pepper, or to taste

4 teaspoons natural yoghurt

1 teaspoon salt

1½ teaspoons garam masala (shop-bought is fine)

1 teaspoon ground coriander

4 tablespoons peeled and very finely chopped onion

1 egg, lightly beaten

Put the turkey in a bowl and combine with the mint, fresh coriander, garlic, cayenne pepper, yoghurt, salt, garam masala, ground coriander and 3 tablespoons of the onions. Mix well. Add the egg and mix again. Put in a plastic bag and refrigerate overnight, or for at least 4–6 hours.

Preheat the oven to 180°C/gas mark 4.

Pat the meat firmly into a 450-g/1-lb loaf tin. Scatter the remaining 1 tablespoon onions over the top and lightly press them in. Bake for 40 minutes.

Heat the grill to its highest setting and place the baked meat under it briefly – until the top is just browned. Unmould, with the onion side on top. Cut into slices and serve, or put the loaf out like a pâté and let people help themselves.

Prawn & Onion Fritters

Known as *bhajia*, *bhaja*, *pakora* and many other names in different parts of India, fritters are an integral part of every single local cuisine in the nation. The flour that is generally used is the protein-rich chickpea flour (though sometimes rice flour is mixed in for extra crunch). That is the constant. After that, anything can be 'frittered' – leaves, roots, fish, roe, vegetables – take your pick. The batter can be thick or thin, spicy or mild – you take your pick again. Most fritters are served with chutneys. I suggest Fresh Green Chutney (see page 237) or Peshawari Red Pepper Chutney (see page 238) here, but if you do not have time, bottled tomato ketchup or a last-minute squeeze of lime juice will suffice.

In India and Pakistan fritters are eaten as a snack with chutneys and tea. In Bangladesh they can be a first course served with rice. In the West they have acquired another life altogether: they are served as starters in restaurants and as canapés with drinks.

Ideally, these fritters, rather like chips, are best eaten as soon as they come out of the frying pan. If that is not possible, make them ahead of time and reheat them in a medium oven for 10 minutes **Makes about 28 fritters; serves 4–6**

100 g/3½ oz chickpea flour

½ teaspoon baking powder

¾ teaspoon salt

freshly ground black pepper

½–¾ teaspoon cayenne pepper

1 teaspoon ground cumin

2 tablespoons peeled and very finely chopped red onion or shallots

2 tablespoons very finely chopped fresh coriander

225 g/½ lb raw, headless prawns, peeled and deveined, cut crossways into 7-mm/⅓-inch pieces, or 180–225 g/ 6–8 oz raw, peeled and cleaned prawns, cut crossways into 7-mm/⅓-inch pieces

olive or rapeseed oil, for frying

Sift the flour, baking powder and salt into a bowl. Very slowly add about 120 ml/4 fl oz water, enough to get a thick batter that drops reluctantly from a spoon. Keep mixing to get rid of all lumps. Add the black pepper, cayenne pepper and cumin. Stir to mix well. Now add the onion, coriander and prawns. Stir to mix.

Pour the oil into a frying pan to a depth of about 2.5 cm/1 inch and set over a medium heat. Give it plenty of time to heat up. Meanwhile, line a baking sheet with kitchen paper.

When the oil is hot (a small piece of batter should sizzle if dropped in), pick up 1 heaped teaspoon of the batter and release it into the hot oil with the help of another teaspoon. Quickly put in enough spoonfuls to use up half the batter. Stir and fry for 6–7 minutes, or until the fritters are a reddish-gold. Remove with a slotted spoon and place on the prepared sheet. Make a second batch in the same way as you made the first. Serve hot.

Fried Whitebait, the Sri Lankan Way

There is nothing quite like sitting at a table by the beach, toes buried in the hot sand, eating these crisp whitebait with a glass of whisky in hand. At least, that is how I love them, but I have also been offered whitebait at a Sri Lankan tea, along with cakes and sandwiches. They were delightful then, too. I love to serve them as a first course. To get the fish nice and crisp, they need to be fried twice. The first frying can be done ahead of time, but the second needs to be done just before eating. They may be served simply as they are, or with a dipping sambol (relish), such as Sri Lankan Coconut Sambol (see page 242) or Sri Lankan Cooked Coconut Chutney (see page 241) **Serves 4**

250 g/9 oz whitebait

¼ teaspoon salt

freshly ground black pepper

¾–1 teaspoon cayenne pepper

2 teaspoons lemon juice

olive or rapeseed oil, for
  deep-frying

140 g/5 oz plain white flour

Wash the whitebait well, then put them in a sieve to drain thoroughly. Using kitchen paper, pat them as dry as you can. Put them in a bowl. Add the salt, black pepper, cayenne pepper and lemon juice. Toss to mix and leave for 15 minutes.

Pour a 5-cm/2-inch depth of oil into a *karhai*, wok or saucepan. Set over medium–low heat for 4–5 minutes. Line a baking sheet with kitchen paper.

Meanwhile, spread the flour out on a large plate. Lay a batch of fish singly on it and roll around to cover. Put the floured fish to one side and repeat this process with the remaining fish. Place all the floured fish in a clean sieve and shake off the excess flour.

When the oil is hot, fry the fish in several batches, allowing about a minute for each batch. Remove with a slotted spoon and spread on the prepared baking sheet. Turn off the heat.

Just before eating, heat the oil again over a medium–high heat. When very hot, fry the fish again in batches for about 3–4 minutes, or until they are golden and crisp. Drain on kitchen paper and serve hot.

Prawns with Garlic & Chillies

This is easily one of my favourite first courses for dinner parties, one that I have served repeatedly over the years. Most of the work – and there is very little of it – can be done in advance, and the last-minute stir-frying, which is the ideal way to cook this, takes only a few minutes. It's possible to do the entire cooking in advance if you wish. Just remember to reheat the prawns over a low flame. I have even served this dish with drinks. I stick a cocktail stick in each prawn and hand out napkins! **Serves 4**

12 raw jumbo prawns, peeled and deveined

⅛ –¼ teaspoon cayenne pepper, or to taste

freshly ground black pepper

¼ teaspoon salt

1 teaspoon finely chopped fresh hot green chillies

2 tablespoons olive, rapeseed or peanut oil

½ teaspoon whole brown or yellow mustard seeds

1 large clove garlic, peeled and finely chopped

15 fresh curry leaves or 10 fresh basil leaves, torn

5 tablespoons grated tomato (see page 267)

Wash the prawns well. Leave in a sieve for a while, then pat dry. Put in a bowl. Add the cayenne pepper, pepper, salt and chillies. Mix well. The prawns may be covered and refrigerated until needed.

Put the oil in a *karhai*, wok or frying pan and set over a medium–high heat. When hot, put in the mustard seeds. As soon as they begin to pop, a matter of seconds, add the garlic and stir once or twice. Quickly put in the prawns and curry leaves. Stir a few times. Add the grated tomato. Stir a few times. Turn the heat down to medium–low and let the prawns cook gently, stirring just until they turn opaque, a matter of 2 or 3 minutes. Serve immediately.

Cold Cucumber Soup

I love to make this soup in the summer, when my garden is bursting with cucumbers and tomatoes. The first time I had it, or a version of it, was in the Maldives. For the soup, the chef had combined south Indian seasonings and the notion of north India's cucumber raita, a yoghurt relish, to fashion a light, cooling soup. I remember sitting in an airy pavilion, the calm blue sea on two sides of me, sipping the soup and thinking, 'This is what heaven must be like.'

While the flavours were easy on the tongue, the soup was complicated to make. I have now simplified it. You could serve it with a dollop of the Quick Yoghurt-rice Garnish on page 33, which is what I love to do **Serves 6–8**

2 tablespoons olive or rapeseed oil

2 tablespoons skinned urad dal or yellow split peas

1 tablespoon whole brown or yellow mustard seeds

2 dried, hot red chillies

15 fresh curry leaves, if available, torn

950 ml/32 fl oz chicken stock

about 2 medium cucumbers, enough to get 750 ml/24 fl oz after peeling and blending, plus some finely diced cucumber for garnishing

¾ teaspoon salt, or to taste

450 ml/15 fl oz natural yoghurt

8 cherry tomatoes, cut into 2-cm/¼-inch dice, for garnishing

Put the oil in a small pan and set over a medium–high heat. When very hot, put in the dal. As soon as it takes on a hint of colour, add the mustard seeds and chillies. As soon as the mustard seeds pop, a matter of seconds, throw in the curry leaves and quickly add the chicken stock. Bring to the boil. Turn the heat down to medium–low and simmer, uncovered, for about 15 minutes, or until the stock is reduced to 750 ml/24 fl oz. Set aside for 3 hours or overnight in the refrigerator, allowing the stock to chill and become infused with the seasonings. Strain.

Peel and roughly dice the cucumbers. Put in a blender and blend finely. You should have about 750 ml/24 fl oz.

Put the salt and yoghurt in a large bowl and whisk lightly so you have a smooth mixture. Slowly whisk in the chicken stock and blended cucumber. Taste for salt, then refrigerate until needed.

To serve, stir the soup well as it tends to separate, and ladle into soup bowls. Sprinkle the diced cucumber and diced tomatoes over the top.

Quick Yoghurt-rice Garnish for Soups

The French drop a dollop of *rouille*, a spicy, garlicky mayonnaise, in the centre of fish soups. It perks them up. Well, this is its Indian incarnation, a quick version of the southern Yoghurt Rice (see page 213), perfect for placing in the centre of not only the preceding Cold Cucumber Soup, but all manner of bean and split-pea soups. I like to serve the soups in old-fashioned soup plates, which are shallower than soup bowls. This way the dollop of garnish stands up and is not drowned

Makes enough garnish for 6–8 servings

about 100 g/3½ oz cooked white rice

4 tablespoons cold milk

4 tablespoons natural yoghurt, lightly beaten

salt and freshly ground black pepper

2 teaspoons olive or rapeseed oil

½ teaspoon whole black or yellow mustard seeds

10 fresh curry leaves, if available, or 5 fresh basil leaves, torn

⅛ teaspoon cayenne pepper

Sprinkle the rice with about 2 tablespoons of water, then cover and heat through, either in a microwave oven for 1 minute or in a small pan. While still hot, add the milk first and then the yoghurt. Mix. Sprinkle lightly with salt and pepper, tasting to make sure it is properly seasoned.

Put the oil in a small pan and set over a medium–high heat. When very hot, put in the mustard seeds. As soon as the seeds begin to pop, a matter of seconds, put in the curry leaves and then the cayenne pepper. Now pour this mixture over the yoghurt rice. Stir to mix.

Put a generous dollop in the centre of each soup plate.

Okra & Swiss Chard Soup

This soup, mellowed with coconut milk, is as delicious as it is surprising in its final blend of silken textures **Serves 6**

3 tablespoons olive or rapeseed oil

1 medium onion, peeled and chopped

1 medium carrot, peeled and chopped

115 g/4 oz green beans, trimmed and coarsely cut up

25 smallish fresh okra, topped and tailed and cut into pieces 7 mm/⅓ inch long

450 g/1 lb Swiss chard, chopped, stems and all

1 teaspoon ground cumin

¼ teaspoon cayenne pepper

1.12 litres/36 fl oz chicken stock

250 ml/8 fl oz coconut milk, from a well-shaken can

salt

Put the oil in a large pan and set over a medium–high heat. When hot, add the onion, carrot, beans and okra. Sauté for 5 minutes. Add the chard, cumin and cayenne pepper. Sauté another 2–3 minutes. Now add half the stock and bring to the boil. Cover, lower the heat and simmer gently for about 25 minutes.

Ladle the soup in batches into a blender and blend until smooth. Return the soup to the pan. Add the remaining stock and the coconut milk. Stir to mix, then taste for salt, adding as much as you need. Reheat before serving.

Red Pepper Soup with Ginger & Fennel

This has always been a favourite soup of mine. I made it very recently with the last of the peppers on my plants. The leaves had shrivelled but the peppers were still hanging on. It was such a cold, damp day that I decided to add some warming ginger to the soup for added comfort **Serves 6**

900 g/2 lb red peppers

4 tablespoons olive or rapeseed oil

1 medium onion, peeled and chopped

1 medium potato, peeled and chopped

2.5-cm/1-inch piece of fresh ginger, peeled and chopped

½ teaspoon whole fennel seeds

¼ teaspoon ground turmeric

1 teaspoon ground cumin seeds

¼ teaspoon cayenne pepper

1.2–1.25 litres/40–45 fl oz chicken or vegetable stock

1 teaspoon salt

5–6 tablespoons single cream

Chop the peppers coarsely, discarding all the seeds.

Put the oil in a large, wide pan and set over a medium–high heat. When hot, put in the peppers, onion, potato, ginger, fennel seeds, turmeric, cumin and cayenne pepper. Stir and fry until all the vegetables just start to brown. Add 600 ml/20 fl oz of the stock and the salt. Stir and bring to a simmer. Cover, lower the heat and simmer gently for 25 minutes.

Ladle the soup in batches into a blender and blend until smooth. Pour the blended soup into a clean pan. Add the remaining stock, thinning the soup as much as you like. Add the cream and mix it in. Adjust the salt as necessary. Reheat before serving.

Gujarati-style Tomato Soup

Gujaratis in western India do not actually drink soups as such. However, they do have many soupy dishes, which are meant to be eaten with flatbreads, rice or spongy, savoury steamed cakes known as *dhoklas*. Here is one such dish. It makes for a gorgeous soup. I serve it with a little dollop of cream and a light sprinkling of ground roasted cumin (see page 263), though these are not essential. In the summer months I make my own tomato purée and use that in the soup. Shop-bought passata works well too. In Gujarat a similar dish, known as *dal dhokli*, is served with home-made noodles in it. I sometimes throw small quantities of cooked pasta bow-ties or even macaroni into the soup. You can do the same if you wish **Serves 4**

3 tablespoons olive or rapeseed oil

⅛ teaspoon ground asafoetida (optional)

½ teaspoon whole brown mustard seeds

½ teaspoon whole cumin seeds

2 tablespoons chickpea flour

1 litre/32 fl oz chicken or vegetable stock or water

500 ml/16 fl oz tomato passata (see page 268)

about 20 fresh curry leaves or 6 fresh basil leaves, torn

¼ teaspoon ground turmeric

⅛–¼ teaspoon cayenne pepper

1 teaspoon salt, or to taste

1½ teaspoons granulated sugar, or to taste

Put the oil in a large pan and set over a medium–high heat. When hot, put in the asafoetida, mustard and cumin seeds. As soon as the seeds begin to pop, a matter of seconds, add the flour. Turn the heat to medium–low. Stir a few times with a whisk until the flour turns a shade darker and is a pale brown.

Slowly add the stock, stirring with a whisk as you go. When well mixed and thick, add the passata, mixing as you do so, then add the curry leaves, turmeric, cayenne pepper, salt and sugar. Bring to the boil. Lower the heat and simmer for 25 minutes.

Turn off the heat and leave the soup in the pan as long as possible so that the spices release more of their flavours. Push through a sieve and reheat before serving.

Tomato-lentil Soup
I make this a lot when tomatoes are in season. It's ideal as a simple, nutritious lunch or first course **Serves 4**

800 g/1¾ lb tomatoes, chopped

100 g/3½ oz red lentils

475 ml/16 fl oz chicken stock or water

1 tablespoon whole coriander seeds

1 teaspoon whole cumin seeds

¼ teaspoon ground turmeric

¼ teaspoon cayenne pepper, or to taste

½ medium onion, peeled and chopped

2.5-cm/1-inch piece of fresh ginger, peeled and chopped

1 handful of fresh coriander

10–15 fresh curry leaves, if available, or 6 fresh basil leaves, torn

1 teaspoon salt

Combine all ingredients except the salt in a pan and bring to a simmer. Cover partially, turn the heat to low and simmer very gently for 1 hour.

Add the salt and mix in. Strain the soup through a coarse sieve, pushing it down with the back of a wooden spoon. Reheat before serving, stirring as you do so.

Red Lentil Curry Soup

Somewhere between the famous Mulligatawny Soup of the Anglo–Indians and the soupy lentil-tomato-pasta dish *dal dholki* of the vegetarians in the western state of Gujarat lies this soup. It is made with red lentils and tomatoes and may be served with a dollop of plain white rice or with some cooked pasta (pappardelle, tagliatelle, macaroni) added to the soup just before it is heated for serving. This soup, plus a salad, makes for a perfect lunch or supper.

There are three simple steps to follow here. First, you boil up the lentils. As they cook, you sauté the seasonings. Then you combine the two and blend them

Serves 4–6

200 g/7 oz red lentils (called masoor dal in Indian shops), well washed and drained

1 litre/32 fl oz chicken stock or water, plus 175 ml/6 fl oz for thinning out

¼ teaspoon ground turmeric

1 medium carrot, peeled and chopped

1 handful of fresh coriander (just rip some off the top of the bunch)

salt

For the seasonings

2 tablespoons olive or rapeseed oil

6 tablespoons peeled and roughly chopped onions

1 teaspoon peeled and finely grated fresh ginger

1 teaspoon ground cumin

1 teaspoon ground coriander

1 teaspoon curry powder

⅛ teaspoon cayenne pepper

about 200 g/7 oz chopped fresh tomatoes

Combine the lentils and first amount of stock in a pan and bring to the boil. Skim off the white froth and add the turmeric, carrot and coriander. Stir, cover partially and turn the heat to low. Cook for 45 minutes.

Meanwhile, put the oil in a frying pan and set over a medium heat. When hot, put in the onions. Stir and fry until they turn brown at the edges. Take the pan off the heat and add the ginger, cumin, coriander, curry powder and cayenne pepper. Return to the heat and stir for 1 minute. Add the tomatoes and 150 ml/5 fl oz water. Cook, stirring now and then, over a medium heat, until the tomatoes are soft. Turn off the heat.

When the lentils have cooked for 45 minutes, empty the contents of the frying pan into the lentil pan, stir, cover and cook over a low heat for 10 minutes, adding salt to taste. Blend the soup, adding the second amount of stock or water to swish out the remains sticking to the blender. Reheat the soup, stirring as you do so.

Peshawari Broth with Mushrooms & Fish

Here is a soup that I was offered on a rather cold day in Pakistan's most famous north-western city, Peshawar. It was a steaming bowl of well-seasoned goat broth in which floated oyster mushrooms and slices of river fish. It was so delicious that I decided to come up with a version myself. I have used beef stock, though lamb stock would do as well. If you cannot get fresh oyster mushrooms, use the canned ones sold by Chinese grocers, or canned straw mushrooms. Just drain and rinse them **Serves 4**

1.3 litres/42 fl oz beef broth/
  stock

½ teaspoon whole cumin seeds

½ teaspoon whole fennel seeds

1 tablespoon whole coriander
  seeds

6 cardamom pods

6 cloves

½ teaspoon whole black
  peppercorns

salt

1 tablespoon olive or
  rapeseed oil

115 g/4 oz fresh oyster
  mushrooms, broken into
  4-cm/1½-inch pieces

1 fresh green bird's eye chilli,
  or about ⅛ teaspoon any
  fresh, hot green chilli, finely
  chopped

225 g/8 oz white fish fillet,
  such as flounder, skinned,
  cut into 2.5 x 5-cm/1 x
  2-inch pieces and sprinkled
  lightly with salt on both sides

4 tablespoons chopped fresh
  coriander

Combine the broth with all the seeds, the cardamom, cloves and peppercorns in a medium pan and bring to the boil. Cover, lower the heat and simmer very gently for 20 minutes. Strain the broth, then return it to the pan. Taste for salt and adjust if necessary.

Put the oil in a non-stick frying pan and set over a medium–high heat. When hot, add the mushrooms and chilli. Stir and sauté for about 2 minutes, or until the mushrooms have softened. Salt lightly and stir again. Transfer to the pan containing the broth.

Just before eating, bring the broth to the boil. Slip in the fish pieces and turn the heat to low. When the fish turns opaque and the broth is simmering, the soup is ready. Sprinkle in the chopped coriander, stir once and serve.

Spinach & Ginger Soup Perfumed with Cloves

Here is a soup that is perfect for cold winter days, the ginger in it providing lasting warmth. Ginger also helps if you have a cold, and acts as a stabiliser for those who suffer from travel sickness. Apart from all its health-giving properties (which Indians always have at the back of their mind), this is a delicious soup that can be served at any meal **Serves 4–6**

1 litre/32 fl oz chicken stock

285 g/10 oz spinach, well washed and coarsely chopped

1 medium carrot, peeled and cut crossways into thick slices

1 medium onion, peeled and coarsely chopped

1 large potato (225–250 g/8–9 oz), peeled and coarsely chopped

½–1 fresh, hot green chilli, chopped (if using a jalapeño, use ¼)

2.5-cm/1-inch piece of fresh ginger, peeled and very finely chopped

2 cloves

10 black peppercorns

salt

120 ml/4 fl oz single cream, plus a little more for drizzling

2 teaspoons lemon juice

In a good-sized pan, combine the stock, spinach, carrot, onion, potato, chilli, ginger, cloves and peppercorns. Bring to the boil. Cover, turn the heat to low and simmer 20 minutes, or until the potatoes are tender.

Blend the soup in batches until smooth. Pour back into the pan through a coarse sieve, adding ¾ teaspoon salt (more if the stock was unsalted), the cream and lemon juice. Mix and bring to the boil over a medium heat, stirring and tasting for balance of seasonings. Drizzle a little cream on top of every serving, if desired.

Chicken Mulligatawny Soup

This is a soup of colonial origin, born in the early days of the Raj and a favourite among the mixed-race Anglo–Indian community of India. All the ingredients and seasonings are completely Indian. It is just the way it is served (in a soup plate) and eaten (with a soup spoon) that is British.

This soup may be served at the start of a meal, or offered as the main course for a Sunday lunch, the way the Anglo–Indians do. At such times, plain rice is served on the side, each diner adding as much as desired to their soup plates. I like to give my guests individual bowls of rice so that a single large bowl of rice does not have to move around the table like a whirling dervish **Serves 4**

3 boneless, skinless chicken thighs (450 g/1 lb in total), cut into 1-cm/½-inch pieces

scant ½ teaspoon salt

freshly ground black pepper

1 teaspoon peeled and finely grated fresh ginger

3 cloves garlic, peeled and crushed

1½ teaspoons ground coriander

1 teaspoon ground cumin

¼ teaspoon cayenne pepper

¼ teaspoon ground turmeric

1 teaspoon hot curry powder

4 tablespoons olive or rapeseed oil

115 g/4 oz chickpea flour, sifted

1.5 litres/48 fl oz chicken stock

3 tablespoons lemon juice

Combine the chicken, salt, pepper, ginger, garlic, coriander, cumin, cayenne pepper, turmeric and curry powder in a bowl. Mix well, cover and set aside for at least 30 minutes, or refrigerate for up to 8 hours.

Put the oil in a pan large enough to hold the stock easily and set over a medium–high heat. When hot, put in all the chicken. Stir and fry for 3–4 minutes, or until the chicken turns white. Add the sifted chickpea flour and continue to stir and fry for about 2 minutes.

Slowly add the chicken stock and 120 ml/4 fl oz water, stirring from the bottom to incorporate whatever is stuck down there. Bring to the boil. Cover, lower the heat and simmer gently for 20 minutes, stirring now and then. Taste for salt, adding some if your stock was unsalted. Stir in the lemon juice.

Fish & Seafood

Indians, Pakistanis, Bangladeshis and Sri Lankans eat much more fish than you might surmise from dining at their restaurants abroad. The countries of southern Asia have long coastlines dotted with fish-market towns selling everything from the smallest of cockles to the largest marlin, kingfish and swordfish – all fresh, hauled in the same day.

From the sea there are red snappers and black groupers to be had, as well as silver pomfrets that might well be steamed in banana leaves or cooked in creamy coconut sauces. There are sardines to put into fiery Kerala curries, and kingfish to be pan-fried with turmeric and chillies. From the estuaries, where rivers meet the sea, there are prawns and crabs to be collected and cooked with mustard seeds or coconut milk. The shad-like *hilsa* swims upstream in some rivers and is wonderful steamed in a mustard sauce or smoked. Mountain streams are well stocked with trout, which anglers deep-fry on site and eat with a salt and Kashmiri chilli powder dip. The rice paddies are filled with catfish and eels, and the mighty rivers of the Gangetic Plain teem with the delicate-fleshed local fish *singhara* and *rahu*. All are fished and eaten.

In many parts of India it is a tradition to rub cut pieces of fish with a little salt and turmeric. The salt firms up the fish so that it does not disintegrate in the pan, and the turmeric acts as an antiseptic. Indians have done this for thousands of years. In Bengal, in eastern India and in Bangladesh a thin sauce made with crushed mustard seeds, chilli powder and turmeric is much loved, while in Kerala, small fish, such as sardines and whitebait, are washed in a lime–water solution, dipped in rice flour and deep-fried. In Pakistan fish rubbed with ajowan seeds (of the thyme family) are roasted briefly in a fiercely hot tandoor oven, and in Sri Lanka you might be served fish perfumed with fennel seeds and poached in coconut milk.

You will find some of these recipes in this chapter, designed for fish available in Western markets.

Fish & Peas in a Fennel-fenugreek Sauce

I used to make this dish with fillets of halibut until the cost made me look at other fish. Now I use cod or hake. They both flake a bit more, but still manage to hold their shape. Salting them ahead of time helps hold them together. I like to use fresh tomatoes, even if out of season, as the flavour is gentler. I grate them (see page 267) as that removes the skin but keeps the seeds. Four medium tomatoes will yield roughly 400 ml/14 fl oz of fresh, light purée, about what you need here. Light and lovely, this is best served with rice. I like to add a dal and perhaps a green, leafy vegetable **Serves 2–3**

450 g/1 lb fillet of cod, hake or halibut, 1–2 cm/½–¾ inch thick

salt

freshly ground black pepper

cayenne pepper

⅛ teaspoon ground turmeric

3 tablespoons mustard, olive or rapeseed oil

⅛ teaspoon ground asafoetida

¼ teaspoon whole mustard seeds

½ teaspoon whole cumin seeds

¼ teaspoon whole fennel seeds

⅛ teaspoon whole fenugreek seeds

3 tablespoons natural yoghurt, preferably 'bio' or Greek

4 medium tomatoes, coarsely grated (see page 267)

140 g/5 oz peas, defrosted if frozen

Sprinkle the fish on both sides with ¼ teaspoon salt, some black pepper, ¼ teaspoon cayenne pepper and the turmeric. Set aside for 30 minutes or longer, refrigerating if necessary.

Put the oil in a frying pan and set over a medium–high heat. When hot, put in the asafoetida, then the mustard, cumin, fennel and fenugreek seeds. As soon as the mustard seeds start to pop, a matter of seconds, add the yoghurt. Stir over a medium–high heat until the yoghurt almost disappears. Add the tomatoes, ¾ teaspoon salt, ¼ teaspoon cayenne pepper and some black pepper. Stir and cook for 5 minutes or until the tomatoes thicken slightly. Add the peas, stir and continue to cook for another minute over a medium heat.

Lay the fish down in this sauce. If there is a thinnish tail end, tuck it under. Spoon the sauce over the fish and bring to a simmer. Cover, leaving the lid slightly ajar, and poach the fish over a medium–low heat, spooning the sauce over now and then, until it is just cooked through, about 7–10 minutes.

Masala Fish Steaks

You can use almost any fish steaks here – salmon, kingfish, cod, haddock, swordfish, salmon trout, pomfret, pompano or tilefish – all depending upon the part of the world you live in. When using the blender, make sure you put the chopped red pepper in first as that will provide the liquid needed to make a paste. If your blender remains stubborn, add a tablespoon or two of water. You could serve this with Courgettes & Yellow Summer Squash with Cumin and Bulgar Pilaf with Peas & Tomato (see pages 152 and 218) **Serves 2–4**

450 g/1 lb fish steaks (see above)

salt

½ large red pepper, seeded and chopped

4 cloves garlic, peeled and chopped

2.5-cm/1-inch piece of fresh ginger, peeled and chopped

¼ teaspoon dried thyme

1 small onion, peeled and chopped

½ teaspoon cayenne pepper

olive or rapeseed oil, for shallow-frying

lime or lemon juice

Sprinkle the fish with ¼ teaspoon salt on both sides and set aside, in the refrigerator if necessary.

Put the red pepper, garlic, ginger, thyme, ¾ teaspoon salt, onion and cayenne pepper into a blender in that order and make a paste.

Put a 5-mm/¼-inch depth of oil in a frying pan and set over a medium–high heat. When hot, add the fish steaks and fry until light brown on both sides. Using a slotted spoon, transfer to a plate.

Remove all but 5 tablespoons of the oil from the pan. Put back on a medium–high heat. When hot, add the paste from the blender. Stir and fry for about 3 minutes, or until the paste seems to dry out. Turn the heat down and fry for another 2 minutes.

Put the fish back in the pan, add 2 tablespoons water and cook through on a very low heat, spooning the sauce over the fish. Squeeze some lime juice over the top and serve.

Grilled Masala Salmon

In India we frequently use a paste of ground mustard seeds. I have simplified matters here and used ready-made Dijon mustard instead. Serve this fish with Basmati Rice with Lentils and South Indian-style Green Beans (see pages 208 and 145) **Serves 2**

⅛ teaspoon salt

¼ teaspoon ground cumin

⅛ teaspoon ground coriander

⅛ teaspoon ground turmeric

¼ teaspoon cayenne pepper

340 g/12 oz skinned salmon fillet

2 tablespoons smooth Dijon mustard

1 tablespoon olive or rapeseed oil

2 teaspoons lemon juice

2 tablespoons finely chopped fresh coriander

Rub the salt, cumin, coriander, turmeric and cayenne pepper all over the salmon fillet. Cover and refrigerate for 1–4 hours.

Preheat the oven to 180°C/gas mark 4, and heat the grill to its highest setting.

Mix the mustard, oil and lemon juice in a small bowl. Add the chopped coriander. Rub this mixture all over the fish and place under the grill, about 13 cm/5 inches from the source of heat. When the top has browned lightly, about 4 minutes, transfer the fish to the oven. Bake for about 10 minutes, or until the fish is cooked through.

Quick-cooked Marinated Halibut

If you are after a superbly elegant, gentle dish, look no further. In a long line of meats and seafood grilled after they have been marinated very simply in a paste of fresh ginger, garlic and chillies, this dish is a great family favourite. Salmon or swordfish may be used instead of halibut. Have the fishmonger remove the skin for you. I like to serve this with Karhai Broccoli (see page 146) and a potato or rice dish   **Serves 4**

560 g/1¼ lb section of skinned halibut fillet, 2–2.5 cm/¾–1 inch thick

½ teaspoon salt

¼ teaspoon ground turmeric

2 teaspoons peeled and finely grated fresh ginger

2 cloves garlic, peeled and crushed

1 tablespoon lemon juice

¼ teaspoon cayenne pepper (more if you prefer)

1 tablespoon rice flour or plain flour

4 tablespoons olive or rapeseed oil

Cut the halibut into 4 segments. Rub the salt and turmeric all over and set aside for 20 minutes.

Meanwhile, combine the ginger, garlic, lemon juice and cayenne pepper in a small bowl. Mix well.

After the fish has sat in the salt mixture for 20 minutes, rub the ginger mixture on all sides, patting it in, then cover and refrigerate for 20–30 minutes.

Preheat the oven to 180°C/gas mark 4. Line a small baking tin with foil and set aside.

Dust the top and bottom of the marinade-covered fish pieces with the flour and pat it in.

Put the oil in a non-stick frying pan and set over a medium–high heat. When hot, put in the fish pieces in a single layer, with one of the floured sides down. Fry until brown, about 1 minute, then turn to brown the other side.

Carefully transfer the fish pieces to the prepared baking tin and place in the oven for 10 minutes, or until just cooked through.

Fish Fillets with a Spicy Green Undercoat

Here I use boneless fish fillets with skin – snapper, mackerel, pollock, red mullet, trout or anything else of modest size. If the fillets are too long, I cut them into more convenient lengths (7.5–10 cm/3–4 inches) so that I can turn them easily in a frying pan. The spicy undercoat is quickly made in a food processor or chopper, though the chopping can be done by hand if you prefer. If you want to keep the meal simple, serve with Potato Chaat and Spinach with Garlic & Cumin (see pages 162 and 169), or a salad **Serves 3–4**

For the undercoating

5 good-sized cherry tomatoes (65 g/2¼ oz), halved

1 tablespoon lemon juice

30 g/1 oz fresh coriander, leaves only

2 bird's eye chillies or ½ a jalapeño chilli, chopped

3 cloves garlic, peeled

4-cm/1½-inch piece of fresh ginger, peeled and chopped

½ teaspoon salt

To cook the fish

450–560 g/1–1¼ lb fish fillets with skin (see above)

140 g/5 oz plain white flour

olive or rapeseed oil, for frying

Combine all the ingredients for the undercoating in a food processor or chopper. Chop until you have a fine, granular sauce. Empty into a large glass or stainless steel bowl. Add the fish fillets and mix well. Set aside for 20–30 minutes, not much longer.

Remove the fish from the marinade, shaking off the liquid, and place in a single layer on a plate. Take the solids from the marinade bowl and pat them all over both sides of the fillets.

Spread the flour out on a large plate. Dip the fillets carefully, one at a time, in the flour, coating both sides, and lay them in a single layer on a fresh plate.

Put a 5-mm/¼-inch depth of oil in a large frying pan or sauté pan and set over a medium–high heat. When hot, slip the fillets into the oil and fry for 3–4 minutes per side, until reddish-brown. Drain on kitchen paper and serve hot.

Salmon in a Bengali Mustard Sauce

Eat this with plain rice and make the sauce as hot as you like. In Bengal the mustard seeds are ground at home, but to make matters simpler I have used shop-bought mustard powder. Halibut may be used instead of salmon. This very traditional dish is best served with Plain Basmati Rice and My Everyday Moong Dal (see pages 201 and 192) plus a green vegetable **Serves 2–3**

340 g/12 oz skinless salmon fillet

salt

ground turmeric

cayenne pepper

1 tablespoon mustard powder

2 tablespoons mustard oil or extra virgin olive oil

¼ teaspoon whole brown mustard seeds

¼ teaspoon whole cumin seeds

¼ teaspoon whole fennel seeds

2 fresh, hot green chillies (bird's eye are best), partially slit

Cut the fish into pieces about 2.5 x 5 cm/1 x 2 inches and rub them evenly with ¼ teaspoon salt, ¼ teaspoon ground turmeric and ¼ teaspoon cayenne pepper. Cover and set aside in the refrigerator for at least 30 minutes or up to 8 hours.

Put the mustard powder in a small bowl with ¼–½ teaspoon cayenne pepper, ¼ teaspoon turmeric and ¼ teaspoon salt. Add 1 tablespoon water and mix to a paste. Add another 7 tablespoons water and mix. Set aside.

Put the oil in a medium frying pan and set over a medium–high heat. When hot, put in the mustard seeds. As soon as they start to pop, a matter of seconds, add the cumin and fennel seeds. Stir once and quickly pour in the mustard paste. Add the chillies, stir and bring to a gentle simmer.

Place the fish pieces in the sauce in a single layer. Simmer gently for about 5 minutes, or until the fish is just cooked through, turning the fish over once and spooning the sauce over it all the time.

Salmon in a Tomato-cream Sauce

I first had this sauce, or one similar to it, in the late 1940s. India had just been partitioned, and a refugee family fleeing from what was to become Pakistan had just opened a small, simple restaurant called Moti Mahal in the centre of Delhi. It basically served foods baked in the clay oven called a tandoor. There was one sauced dish, however, Chicken Makhani. A tandoor-roasted chicken was cut up with a cleaver and then heated in this tomatoey, buttery, creamy sauce. I have always loved the sauce. Over the years I have played around with it, using it with prawns and now with salmon. Serve with Swiss Chard with Ginger & Garlic (see page 148) and Rice Pilaf with Almonds & Sultanas (see page 203). **Serves 4**

675 g/1½ lb skinned salmon fillet, from the centre of the fish (where it is thickest)

¼ teaspoon salt

freshly ground black pepper

⅛ teaspoon ground turmeric

⅛ teaspoon cayenne pepper

For the sauce

300 ml/10 fl oz tomato passata (see page 268)

300 ml/10 fl oz single cream

1 teaspoon salt

1 teaspoon caster sugar

1 teaspoon garam masala

1 teaspoon ground cumin

1 tablespoon lemon juice

⅛ teaspoon cayenne pepper

2 tablespoons chopped fresh coriander

To cook the fish

1 tablespoon olive or rapeseed oil

½ teaspoon whole cumin seeds

Cut the salmon lengthways down the centre, then crossways to make 8 pieces. Season with the salt, pepper, turmeric and cayenne pepper on all sides and rub them into the fish. Place in a plastic bag and refrigerate for 1 hour or longer.

Combine all the ingredients for the sauce and mix well. (This can be made up to a day in advance and refrigerated until needed.)

To cook the fish, put the oil in a frying pan and set over a medium heat. When hot, put in the cumin seeds. When the seeds have sizzled for 10 seconds, pour in the sauce. Stir and bring to a simmer.

Place all the fish pieces in the sauce in a single layer and cook, spooning the sauce over the fish. After a minute, turn the fish over and reduce the heat to medium–low. Continue to cook, spooning the sauce over the top, for 3–4 minutes, or until the fish has cooked through.

Bangladeshi Fish Curry

In Bangladesh the basic diet is fish and rice. However, it is not fish from the Bay of Bengal, the sea that rules their shores. In fact, they hardly touch that. What they love is fresh-water fish that comes from their estuaries, rivers, lakes and ponds. Since local Bangladeshi fish are unavailable to most of us, I have adapted this recipe to use fillet of flounder. One of the common local seasonings is an aromatic lime leaf very similar to the kaffir lime leaf of Thailand. If you cannot get that, use fresh curry leaves or, failing that, fresh basil leaves. Serve with plain rice, a dal and a vegetable or salad. **Serves 4**

450–560 g/1–1¼ lb fillet of flounder (2 large fillets are ideal)

salt

1½ teaspoons peeled and crushed garlic

1½ teaspoons peeled and very finely grated fresh ginger

¼ teaspoon ground turmeric

½ teaspoon cayenne pepper

1 teaspoon sweet red paprika

3 tablespoons olive or mustard oil

30 g/1 oz peeled and finely sliced shallots

3 freshly torn kaffir lime leaves, or 10 lightly crushed curry leaves, or 5 torn fresh basil leaves

Put the flounder fillets on a work surface. Sprinkle ¼ teaspoon salt on both sides of them. Cut an 8-cm/3-inch portion off the tail end of each fillet. Now cut the thick part of the fillets in half lengthways, and then crossways into 8-cm/3-inch segments. Set all the pieces aside as you prepare the sauce.

Combine the garlic, ginger, turmeric, cayenne pepper, paprika and ¼ teaspoon salt in a bowl. Add 3 tablespoons water. Mix well to make a paste.

Put the oil into a very large frying pan or sauté pan (a 30-cm/12-inch diameter is ideal) and set over a medium heat. When hot, put in the shallots. Stir and fry until they are lightly browned. Now put in the spice paste. Stir and fry for 1 minute. Add 250 ml/8 fl oz water and the kaffir lime leaves. Stir and bring to a simmer. Simmer on a low heat for 1 minute. Turn off the heat.

Just before serving, bring the sauce to a simmer over a low heat. Lay the fish pieces in the sauce in a single layer. Cook for 1 minute, then carefully turn the fish over. Cook for another 2–3 minutes, spooning the sauce over the top, until the fish is just done.

Kerala-style Fish Curry

Although I use wild sea bass here, you can use whatever fish looks good and fresh – haddock, halibut, salmon (steaks or thick fillet pieces), kingfish steaks or even mackerel pieces. This is a creamy curry best eaten with rice. In Kerala it looks red from all the hot chilli powder in it, but I have softened the heat with some paprika, which also helps to add the colour. Serve with Plain Jasmine Rice and South Indian-style Green Beans (see pages 211 and 145) **Serves 2–4**

450–560g/1–1¼ lb wild sea bass fillet with skin, 1–2 cm/½–¾ inch thick, cut crossways into 7.5-cm/3-inch segments

salt

2 tablespoons olive or rapeseed oil

65 g/2½ oz peeled and very finely sliced shallots

1 teaspoon peeled and finely grated fresh ginger

1 large clove garlic, peeled and crushed

½ teaspoon ground turmeric

½ teaspoon cayenne pepper, or to taste

1 tablespoon sweet red paprika

freshly ground black pepper

1 tablespoon lemon juice

120 ml/4 fl oz coconut milk, from a well-shaken can

Spread the fish pieces out and sprinkle ½ teaspoon salt on both sides. Set aside as you prepare the sauce.

Put the oil into a frying pan and set over a medium–high heat. When hot, put in the shallots. Stir and fry until they just start to brown at the edges. Add the ginger and garlic. Stir for 1 minute. Now add 250 ml/8 fl oz water, the turmeric, cayenne pepper, paprika, lots of black pepper, the lemon juice and ½ teaspoon salt. Bring to a simmer. Turn heat to low and simmer gently for 5 minutes, stirring now and then. Add the coconut milk and mix it in. Bring the sauce back to a simmer.

Put the fish pieces in the pan in a single layer and cook over a medium–low heat, spooning the sauce over them until they are poached, 5–10 minutes.

Sri Lankan Fish Curry

In Sri Lanka, an island nation, fish is a staple. It is used in salads, as a stuffing for savoury pastries, as a flavouring in relishes, as a snack food with drinks, and, of course, in hundreds of curries. This particular curry was served to me for breakfast on a sunny patio at Castlereigh, a former tea planter's home turned boutique hotel, along with fresh rice noodles and good, hot tea. On that cool morning in the mountains nothing could have tasted finer. Almost any fish may be used here – swordfish, salmon, pompano, sole, haddock, kingfish, mackerel – as long as it is firm and holds its shape. I have used swordfish. Serve with Plain Jasmine Rice and Gujarati-style Okra (see pages 211 and 159). **Serves 2–3**

450 g/1 lb boneless swordfish, 2–2.5 cm/¾–1 inch thick

salt

3 tablespoons olive or rapeseed oil

¼ teaspoon whole brown mustard seeds

¼ teaspoon whole fennel seeds

85 g/3 oz peeled and finely chopped red onion

1 clove garlic, peeled and chopped

15–20 fresh curry leaves or 10 fresh basil leaves, torn

1 medium tomato, chopped

⅛ teaspoon ground turmeric

¼–½ teaspoon cayenne pepper

120 ml/4 fl oz coconut milk, from a well-shaken can

Remove the skin of the swordfish and cut it crossways into as many pieces as there are diners. Sprinkle lightly with ¼ teaspoon salt on both sides.

Put the oil in a frying pan and set over a medium–high heat. When hot, put in the mustard seeds. As soon as they begin to pop, a matter of seconds, put in the fennel seeds and then the onion. Stir and fry over a medium heat until the onion softens a bit, about 2–3 minutes. Add the garlic and curry leaves. Stir for another minute. Now add the tomato, turmeric and cayenne pepper. Stir for 1 minute. Add 120 ml/4 fl oz water and ½ teaspoon salt. Stir and bring to a simmer. Cover, turn the heat to low and cook gently for 10 minutes.

Put the fish into this sauce and cook over a medium–low heat for 3–4 minutes, or until one side of the fish turns opaque. Turn the fish over. Add the coconut milk, stir the sauce gently and bring to a simmer again on a medium heat, spooning the sauce over the fish. When the fish turns opaque all the way through, it is done.

Fish in a Fennel-flavoured Curry Sauce

Versions of this fish curry are eaten all along India's long coastline. I like to make it with fillets of Spanish mackerel, but any mackerel or kingfish, indeed, any fish that does not flake too easily, will do. This is perfect with rice. Add a green vegetable and a salad as well **Serves 2–3**

340 g/12 oz Spanish mackerel fillets, with skin

salt

2 teaspoons peeled and finely grated fresh ginger

1 teaspoon peeled and finely crushed garlic

¼–½ teaspoon cayenne pepper, or more if desired

2 teaspoons sweet red paprika

freshly ground black pepper

¼ teaspoon ground turmeric

1 tablespoon lemon juice

2 tablespoons olive or rapeseed oil

¼ teaspoon whole fennel seeds

3 tablespoons peeled and finely chopped shallots or red onion

4–6 tablespoons coconut milk, from a well-shaken can, or single cream

Cut the fish crossways into 8-cm/3-inch segments. Rub about ⅛ teaspoon salt on both sides of the fish and set aside.

Combine the ginger, garlic, cayenne pepper, paprika, black pepper, turmeric, lemon juice and ½ teaspoon salt in a small bowl. Mix.

Put the oil in a frying pan, preferably non-stick, and set over a medium–high heat. When hot, put in the fennel seeds and, a few seconds later, the shallots. Reduce the heat to medium. Stir and sauté the shallots until they soften slightly. Now add the seasonings from the bowl. Stir for 1 minute. Add 250 ml/8 fl oz water, stir and bring to a simmer. Reduce the heat to low and simmer gently, uncovered, for 7–8 minutes. Add the coconut milk or cream. Stir and bring to a simmer again.

Slip the fish pieces into the sauce, skin side down, in a single layer. Keep spooning the sauce over them and cook gently for 6–7 minutes, or until they become opaque.

Stir-fried Squid with Mustard Seeds

Squid is now available cleaned and ready to cook. All you have to do is cut it up as you desire. It is very simple to cook if you know its idiosyncrasies. As it can get tough very easily, you either have to cook squid very fast for 1–2 minutes on a very high heat, or else stew it slowly and gently for at least 45 minutes. The former results in a firm texture, while the latter makes the flesh pliable and soft. The next two recipes give examples of both techniques. Here is a quick stir-fry. Serve it with Plain Jasmine Rice and Corn with Aromatic Seasonings (see pages 211 and 149) **Serves 3–4**

450 g/1 lb cleaned squid

2 cloves garlic, peeled and crushed

1 teaspoon salt

4 tablespoons well-chopped fresh coriander

¼–½ teaspoon cayenne pepper

1 tablespoon chickpea flour, rice flour or plain white flour

10–15 fresh curry leaves or 6 fresh basil leaves, torn

3 tablespoons olive or rapeseed oil

½ teaspoon whole brown mustard seeds

2 whole dried hot red chillies

1 tablespoon lemon juice

freshly ground black pepper

Cut the bodies of the squid crossways into rings 5 mm/¼ inch thick, and separate the tentacles, cutting up those that seem very long. Wash well, drain in a colander and pat dry. Combine the squid, garlic, salt, coriander, cayenne pepper, flour and curry leaves in a bowl. Mix well and set aside for 15 minutes.

Put the oil in a non-stick frying pan and set over a medium–high heat. When hot, put in the mustard seeds. As soon as they start to pop, a matter of seconds, put in the chillies. They will quickly darken. Now put in the squid and spice mixture from the bowl. Stir and fry over a high heat for 1½–2 minutes. Turn off the heat. Add the lemon juice and black pepper. Stir and serve.

Squid Curry

Make this curry as fiery as you like. That is how it is preferred in many parts of southern India. This is generally served with plain rice or with the thin, fresh rice noodles known as *idiappam*. I have given a method of preparing dried rice sticks, sold in Thai and Vietnamese markets, on page 219 (see Thin Rice Noodles.) They are the closest to the Indian noodles. I have also been known to serve this curry over thin spaghettini or angel hair pasta   **Serves 3–4**

450 g/1 lb cleaned squid (see box above)

2 tablespoons olive or rapeseed oil

½ teaspoon whole brown mustard seeds

1 medium onion, peeled and cut into fine half-rings

15 fresh curry leaves or 10 fresh basil leaves, torn

1 teaspoon peeled and finely grated fresh ginger

1 clove garlic, peeled and crushed

1 tablespoon hot curry powder

2 tablespoons tomato purée

¾ teaspoon salt

1 tablespoon lemon juice

Cut the bodies of the squid crossways into rings 5 mm/¼ inch thick, and separate the tentacles, cutting up those that seem very long. Wash well and leave to drain in a colander.

Put the oil in a frying pan and set over a medium–high heat. When hot, put in the mustard seeds. As soon as they start to pop, a matter of seconds, put in the onion and the curry leaves. Stir and fry until the onions just start to brown at the edges. Add the ginger, garlic and curry powder. Stir for 1 minute. Add the tomato purée and stir a few times. Now add 475 ml/16 fl oz water, the salt, lemon juice and squid. Stir and bring to a simmer over a gentle heat. Cover and simmer, stirring now and then, for about 45 minutes, or until the squid is tender.

Goan Prawn Curry

Goa, on India's west coast, is a tropical haven for tourists, who cannot get enough of its easy ways, sun and sand. Strangely enough, some of Goa's best food is not found in expensive resorts but in thatched shacks right by the sea. The fish is always fresh, and there is usually nothing to beat the fiery prawn curry served with a mound of short-grain local rice. Serve with Plain Jasmine Rice (see page 211) and a vegetable or salad of your choice **Serves 4**

2 tablespoons olive or rapeseed oil

2 medium shallots, peeled and finely chopped

¼ teaspoon cayenne pepper, or more if desired

2 teaspoons sweet red paprika

½ teaspoon freshly ground black pepper

¼ teaspoon ground turmeric

300 ml/10 fl oz coconut milk, from a well-shaken can (any remaining milk can be frozen for future use)

450 g/1 lb large or medium raw prawns, peeled and deveined, or 340 g/12 oz raw, headless prawns, peeled and deveined

½ teaspoon salt

1–2 teaspoons lemon juice

Put the oil in a frying pan or sauté pan and set over a medium heat. When hot, put in the shallots. Stir and fry until they turn light brown. Take the pan off the heat and add the cayenne pepper, paprika, black pepper and turmeric. Stir once or twice, then put the pan back on the heat. Add the coconut milk and bring to a simmer, stirring to mix. Reduce the heat to low. Put in the prawns, salt and lemon juice. Stir and cook just until the prawns turn opaque.

Spicy Prawn Stir-fry (*Bhuni Jhinga*)

Here is a very quick way to stir-fry prawns so that they are encrusted with spices. They are hot, sour and utterly delicious. The dish may be served as a first course, as a light lunch with a salad, or as part of a larger Indian meal. Serve with Sri Lankan Rice with Fresh Coriander & Lemon Grass and Mushroom & Pea Curry (see pages 205 and 158)   **Serves 4**

450 g/1 lb medium-sized raw prawns, peeled and deveined or 340 g/12 oz medium-sized raw, headless prawns, peeled and deveined

¼ teaspoon ground turmeric

⅛–¼ teaspoon cayenne pepper, or to taste

1 teaspoon ground coriander

½ teaspoon ground cumin

¼ teaspoon salt

2 tablespoons olive, rapeseed or peanut oil

¼ teaspoon whole brown or yellow mustard seeds

¼ teaspoon whole cumin seeds

1 large clove garlic, peeled and chopped

1½ teaspoons lemon juice

Wash the prawns well. Leave in a sieve for a while, then pat dry and put in a bowl. Add the turmeric, cayenne pepper, coriander, cumin and salt. Mix well.

Put the oil in a frying pan and set over a medium–high heat. When hot, put in the mustard and cumin seeds. As soon as the mustard seeds begin to pop, a matter of seconds, add the garlic and stir once or twice. Quickly put in the prawns and stir once or twice. Turn the heat down immediately to medium–low and let the prawns cook gently, stirring as they do so, until they are just cooked through, 2 or 3 minutes. Add the lemon juice and toss to mix. Serve immediately.

Mussels in a Creamy Coconut Sauce

Here is a dish much beloved by my husband and children. Medium-sized clams may be substituted for the mussels. You can serve this as a first course or main course, or as a light lunch with a salad. Indians eat this curry with rice, but the mussels can be served by themselves in individual bowls **Serves 2–4**

900 g/2 lb medium-sized mussels

2 tablespoons olive or rapeseed oil

½ teaspoon whole brown mustard seeds

1 good-sized onion (about 180 g/6 oz), peeled and finely chopped

1 teaspoon peeled and finely grated fresh ginger

1 teaspoon garlic, peeled and crushed

1 x 400-ml/14-fl oz can coconut milk, well shaken

2 teaspoons ground cumin seeds

¼ teaspoon cayenne pepper

¾ teaspoon salt

15 fresh curry leaves or 10 fresh basil leaves, torn

4 tablespoons finely chopped fresh coriander

2 fresh green chillies (bird's eye are ideal), partially slit

1 tablespoon lemon juice

Scrub the mussels well with a brush, discarding those that remain open even after they are tapped. Pull off any stringy beards.

Put the oil in a large pan and set over a medium–high heat. When hot, put in the mustard seeds. As soon as they start to pop, a matter of seconds, put in the onion and reduce the heat to medium. Stir and cook for 4–5 minutes, or until the onions have softened. Add the ginger and garlic. Stir for 1 minute. Now add the coconut milk, 250 ml/8 fl oz water and all the remaining ingredients. Stir and bring to a simmer. Cook gently, uncovered, stirring now and then, for 5 minutes. (This much can be done ahead of time.)

Add all the mussels and bring to the boil over a medium–high heat. Cover and cook rapidly for 5 minutes, or until all the mussels have opened.

Eggs & Poultry

I love eggs… in every form. There is nothing finer than a soft-boiled egg perched in an eggcup, ready to be eaten with a mixture of salt, pepper and a tiny bit of ground roasted cumin seeds. Or poached eggs served over Potatoes with Cumin & Mustard Seeds (see page 168). Then there are Indian omelettes and scrambled eggs. Every household makes these its own way: some add onions; some put in tomatoes; ginger, turmeric, cumin seeds or mustard seeds can be added; certain flavourings, fresh coriander and fresh green or red chillies, seem to be constants.

Whenever my friend Ismail Merchant, the late film producer, flew into town he would call up and say, 'Come over for dinner.' The fact that his cupboard was completely bare and his refrigerator mostly empty from his weeks abroad did not faze him one bit. He bought some eggs and made an egg curry, which he served with rice, his mother's mango pickle and some salad. What more could one want? Egg curries generally require nothing more than hard-boiled eggs, a few spices and something to provide a sauce, such as tomatoes or coconut milk.

Rather like property, the value of chicken goes up and down. And I do not mean its price, though that is connected. Chicken, which is native to the Indian subcontinent, was once a special treat, reserved for festive occasions. Such was the case when I was growing up in India.

Chicken was expensive. Then came the era of battery farms, with birds all cooped up and fed chemicals and medicines so that they would grow plump fast and not die of diseases. The price of chicken fell, and so did its status. Now better-quality, hormone-free, organic and free-range chickens are being sold, we can serve chicken again at our dinner parties!

Indians eat a lot of chicken, and have done so over the last few thousand years. Most restaurants now sell tandoori chicken, which is roasted in a clay oven. This is a relatively new dish from the north-west that began swooping down to the rest of the nation in the late 1940s, but traditional chicken curries have retained their hold. In western Goa chicken may be cooked with garlic, onion and a little bit of vinegar; in Bombay with apricots; in northern cities, such as Delhi, it may be stewed with spinach and cardamom; in the east it might be cooked in yoghurt with cinnamon, and in the south with mustard seeds, curry leaves and coconut milk.

Indians traditionally remove the skin before cooking chicken. They probably feel that spices penetrate better and that somehow the chicken is cleaner. I go both ways; it depends upon the recipe.

Hunters love their duck and quail. During the winter hunting season, these birds were invariably on our table at the start of each week after a busy weekend (men only) of *shikar* (the hunt).

Soft-boiled Eggs with Seasoned Salt

We all love these in our family. We serve them in eggcups with a small dish of seasoned salt on the side. I like to have the eggs with toast 'soldiers', perfect for dunking into the yolk **Serves 1–2**

2 eggs

1 tablespoon sea salt

freshly ground black pepper

½ teaspoon ground roasted cumin seeds (see page 263)

Bring a saucepan of water to the boil – just enough to cover the eggs. Turn the heat down so the water is simmering gently. Using a spoon, lower the eggs into the water one at a time. Set your timer for 4 minutes if you want the whites soft, 5–5½ minutes if you want the whites almost set and 6 minutes if you want them completely set.

Meanwhile, combine the salt, pepper and cumin and put them into a small bowl or salt-cellar.

As soon as the eggs are done, put them in eggcups and serve immediately with the seasoned salt on the side.

Poached Eggs over Vegetables

I like to poach my eggs in a frying pan. I break them into the pan rather like fried eggs, laying them next to each other, only instead of oil, I use simmering water. I serve them over well-spiced Indian vegetables, whatever I am in the mood for. I cook the vegetables in advance, sometimes using leftovers from the day before. The eggs can be served over Potatoes with Cumin & Mustard Seeds, or Corn with Aromatic Seasonings, or even Swiss Chard with Ginger & Garlic (see pages 168, 149 and 148) **Serves 2**

4 eggs

Use a non-stick frying pan that will hold 4 eggs with ease. A 23-cm/9-inch pan is ideal, though one a little bit larger or smaller will do. Put about 2 cm/¾ inch water in the pan and bring it to a low simmer. Break the eggs into the water so that they lie side by side. Let them cook gently until the whites are almost set. Turn off the heat and cover very loosely. Allow the eggs to set to the consistency you like, watching them carefully. Separate the eggs and, using a slotted spatula, place them on the chosen cooked vegetable.

Two-egg Masala Omelette

In our house we all like different types of omelette, so we tend to make our own. This is how I make mine. Indians generally eat their omelettes with sliced bread, toast or Parathas (see page 225) **Serves 1**

2 eggs, lightly beaten

salt

freshly ground black pepper

1 tablespoon olive or rapeseed oil

⅛ teaspoon whole brown mustard seeds

1/16 teaspoon whole cumin seeds

1 teaspoon peeled and finely chopped shallot or red onion

3 cherry tomatoes, quartered

dash of cayenne pepper or crushed red pepper

1 tablespoon finely chopped fresh coriander

Season the eggs lightly with salt and pepper.

Put the oil into a 15–18-cm/6–7-inch frying pan, preferably non-stick, and set over a medium–high heat. When hot, put in the mustard and cumin seeds. As soon as the mustard seeds pop, a matter of seconds, reduce the heat to medium–low. Put in the shallot and stir once or twice. Quickly add the tomatoes, cayenne pepper, coriander and a dash of salt and pepper. Stir and cook about a minute, or until the tomatoes have softened a bit.

Stir the beaten eggs and add them to the pan. Quickly mix everything together, then let the mixture spread out to the edges of the pan. Cover until the mixture is almost set.

To serve, fold the omelette, bringing the left side slightly past the centre, then folding the right side over the left. Turn the omelette over, pressing down with the spatula for a few seconds. Slide on to a plate and serve immediately.

Indian Scrambled Eggs

Here is our family's most beloved Sunday breakfast/brunch dish. I prepare all the ingredients beforehand and then scramble the eggs as we are sitting down to eat. The asafoetida imparts a truffle-like aroma, but you could leave it out if you wish. Serve this with slices of French or Italian bread, with toast, or with any of the flatbreads in this book (see pages 222, 224 and 225)   **Serves 4–6**

3 tablespoons olive or rapeseed oil

1/16 teaspoon ground asafoetida

1/4 teaspoon whole brown mustard seeds

1/4 teaspoon whole cumin seeds

1–2 teaspoons finely chopped fresh, hot green chilli

15–20 fresh curry leaves, if available, torn

4 medium-sized mushrooms, chopped small

1 tablespoon peeled and finely chopped red onion or shallot

2 teaspoons peeled and finely grated fresh ginger

8–10 cherry tomatoes, chopped

3 tablespoons chopped fresh coriander

12 eggs, beaten

scant 1/2 teaspoon salt, or to taste

freshly ground black pepper

Put the oil in a large frying pan, preferably non-stick and set over a medium–high heat. When hot, put in the asafoetida, mustard and cumin seeds. As soon as the mustard seeds begin to pop, a matter of seconds, put in the chilli, curry leaves and mushrooms. Stir once or twice, then add the onion. Stir a few times and add the ginger and tomatoes. Stir a few times and add the coriander, eggs, salt and pepper. Now just stir to mix and scramble the eggs to the doneness you like, always scraping from the bottom.

Egg Curry

Here is a very easy-to-prepare egg curry. As the sauce is made in the blender, I call it a blender curry. If you like, 2–3 medium-sized boiled, diced potatoes (2-cm/¾-inch dice are best) may be added to the sauce at the same time as the eggs. Serve with rice or any of the three flatbreads in this book (see pages 222, 224 and 225). You could also have the curry with French or Italian bread **Serves 4–6**

4 tablespoons natural yoghurt

4 medium tomatoes (about 560 g/1¼ lb), chopped

3 tablespoons chickpea flour

2.5-cm/1-inch piece of fresh ginger, peeled and chopped

3 teaspoons hot curry powder

1¼–1½ teaspoons salt

2 tablespoons olive or rapeseed oil

½ teaspoon whole cumin seeds

½ teaspoon whole mustard seeds

¼ teaspoon whole fennel seeds

8–12 hard-boiled eggs, peeled and left whole

Put 250 ml/8 fl oz water into a blender followed by the yoghurt, tomatoes, flour, ginger, curry powder and salt in that order. Blend for at least 2 minutes, or until you have a smooth sauce.

Put the oil into a wide pan and set over a medium–high heat. When hot, put in the cumin and mustard seeds. As soon as the mustard seeds begin to pop, a matter of seconds, put in the fennel seeds. Wait about 5 seconds, then take the pan off the heat. Pour in 250 ml/8 fl oz water and then the curry sauce from the blender. Stir and put the pan back on a medium heat. Bring the sauce to a simmer, stirring all the time. Cover, turn the heat to very low and simmer gently for 15 minutes, stirring now and then. Add the hard-boiled eggs and heat them through. Serve immediately.

Chicken Karhai with Mint

This dish takes its named from the utensil in which it is made – the *karhai*, an Indian wok. I like dark meat, and prefer chicken thighs here, but lovers of white meat may use boned and skinned chicken breasts. Serve with rice or flatbreads, and perhaps the Mushroom & Pea Curry (see page 158) on the side. You could also serve this cold, and even take it along on a picnic   **Serves 4**

For the marinade

560 g/1¼ lb boned and skinned chicken thighs, cut into 2-cm/¾-inch pieces

1 teaspoon salt

freshly ground black pepper

½ teaspoon ground cumin

1 teaspoon ground coriander

1½ tablespoons lemon juice

½ teaspoon cayenne pepper

1 teaspoon garam masala, home-made (see page 264) or shop-bought

1 teaspoon peeled and finely grated fresh ginger

1 tablespoon olive or rapeseed oil

To cook the chicken

3 tablespoons olive or rapeseed oil

100 g/3½ oz peeled and chopped onions

3 tablespoons chopped fresh mint

Combine all the marinade ingredients in a non-reactive (ceramic, glass or stainless steel) bowl. Mix, cover and set aside in the refrigerator for at least 30 minutes, or as long as overnight.

Put the 3 tablespoons oil in a *karhai*, wok or large frying pan and set over a medium–high heat. When hot, add the onions. Stir-fry for 1 minute. Add the chicken and all its marinade. Stir-fry for another 3 minutes, or until the chicken is just cooked through. Add the mint and stir-fry for a few seconds.

Stir-fried Chicken Breast with Black Pepper & Green Chillies

I like to use bird's eye chillies here, but any fresh, hot green chillies will do. Use only as much of the larger chillies as you think you can handle. I often make this when I am in a hurry as it cooks fast. Serve with any rice dish. I like it with the Tomato Pullao (see page 206). This is also great to take on picnics or to serve at a summer lunch: fill pita bread pockets with this, spoon in a little Fresh Green Chutney (see page 237) and eat! **Serves 2–3**

340 g/12 oz boneless, skinless chicken breast, cut into 2-cm/¾-inch pieces

1 clove garlic, peeled and crushed

1 teaspoon peeled and very finely grated fresh ginger

½ teaspoon salt

2 teaspoons lemon juice

generous amount of freshly ground black pepper

⅛ teaspoon cayenne pepper

2 tablespoons olive or rapeseed oil

4 cardamom pods

½ medium onion, peeled and finely chopped

1–2 fresh bird's eye chillies, chopped

2 tablespoons natural yoghurt

⅛ teaspoon ground turmeric

Combine the chicken, garlic, ginger, salt, lemon juice, black pepper and cayenne pepper in a bowl. Mix well.

Put the oil in a frying pan or wok and set over a medium–high heat. When hot, put in the cardamom pods. Stir once and put in the onion and chillies. Stir and fry until the onion pieces turn brown at the edges. Add 1 tablespoon of yoghurt and stir it until it disappears. Add the second tablespoon of yoghurt. When it disappears, add the turmeric and the seasoned chicken. Stir and fry for 1 minute. Add 2 tablespoons water, cover and turn the heat to low. Cook for 2 minutes, or until the chicken is cooked through.

Remove the cover. Turn the heat up and let all the liquid evaporate, stirring as this happens.

Stir-fried Chettinad Chicken

A dish from the south-eastern state of Tamil Nadu, this quick stir-fry has all the wonderful spices used in the cooking of the Chettiyars, a trading community – lots of black pepper, fennel seeds, mustard seeds, cinnamon and the split peas called urad dal. (Yellow split peas may be substituted for this last ingredient, which is used here in a very southern way, as a seasoning.) This dish has a 30-minute marinating period, but it cooks in about 7 minutes. It is a good idea to have all the spices measured out and ready for the stir-fry as that is a fast procedure. I like this dish with Basmati Rice with Lentils (see page 208) and a green vegetable **Serves 4**

560 g/1¼ lb boned and skinned chicken thighs (if you prefer light meat, skinned and boned breasts may be substituted)

1 teaspoon salt

freshly ground black pepper

1 teaspoon peeled and finely grated fresh ginger

¼ teaspoon ground turmeric

¼ teaspoon cayenne pepper

4 tablespoons olive or rapeseed oil

½ teaspoon whole brown mustard seeds

½ teaspoon skinned urad dal or yellow split peas

½ teaspoon whole fennel seeds

2 x 5-cm/2-inch cinnamon sticks

2 hot dried red chillies

20 fresh curry leaves, if available, or 8 fresh basil leaves, torn

½ medium onion, peeled and chopped

8 cherry tomatoes, halved

Cut the chicken into 2-cm/¾-inch pieces and put in a bowl. Add the salt, a very generous quantity of black pepper, the ginger, turmeric and cayenne pepper. Mix well, cover and refrigerate for 30 minutes.

Put the oil in a wok or large frying pan and set over a medium–high heat. When hot, put in the mustard seeds, urad dal, fennel seeds, cinnamon sticks and red chillies. As soon as the mustard seeds pop, a matter of seconds, put in the curry leaves, onion and chicken. Stir and fry for about 5 minutes, or until the chicken has cooked through and browned. Add the tomatoes and stir for 30 seconds. Check for salt, adding a light sprinkling if needed.

Goan-style Chicken Moelho

There is a whole family of Goan meat and chicken dishes, including the famous *vindaloos*, that have in common the use of garlic, vinegar and hot chillies – all of which help preserve the food and give it a slightly 'pickled' feel. The chillies used in Goa are often of the Kashmiri variety, which impart a very red colour but are of medium heat. Each dish requires rather a lot of them, and ends up being very hot and very red. I have used a mixture of cayenne pepper and paprika. You can add more cayenne if you like. In Goa this is eaten with partially milled red-hulled rice. You could serve it with Plain Brown Rice, Plain Jasmine Rice or Coconut Rice (see pages 214, 211 and 212). Add vegetables and salads **Serves 3–4**

1½ teaspoons whole cumin seeds

1 teaspoon whole brown mustard seeds

560 g/1¼ lb boneless, skinless chicken thighs, all excess fat discarded and cut into 2.5-cm/1-inch pieces

¾–1 teaspoon cayenne pepper

2 teaspoons sweet red paprika

½ teaspoon ground turmeric

1¼ teaspoons salt

1 tablespoon red wine vinegar, plus a little more, as needed

4 cloves garlic, peeled and crushed

3 tablespoons olive or rapeseed oil

1 medium onion, peeled and cut into fine half-rings

Put the cumin seeds and mustard seeds into a clean coffee-grinder and grind finely.

In a non-reactive (ceramic, glass or stainless steel) bowl, combine the chicken, cumin-mustard mixture, cayenne pepper, paprika, turmeric, salt, 1 tablespoon vinegar and the garlic. Mix well with the hands, cover and set aside for 1–2 hours, refrigerating if needed.

Put the oil in a large frying pan, preferably non-stick, and set over a medium–high heat. When hot, put in the onions. Stir and fry until they become translucent, about 4–5 minutes. Keep stirring and frying for another 2 minutes, or until the onions brown a bit. Now add all the marinated chicken. Stir and fry for another 7–8 minutes or until the chicken turns opaque and browns a bit. Add 120 ml/4 fl oz water and another 2 teaspoons vinegar. Bring to the boil. Cover, reduce the heat and simmer gently for 5 minutes. Check the salt, adding more if needed.

Chicken with Okra

This very home-style Indian dish can best be compared to a New Orleans gumbo. It is the okra and tomatoes that give it the gumbo feel, but the seasonings are very north Indian. Serve it with rice or Indian breads **Serves 2–3**

450 g/1 lb boneless, skinless chicken thighs cut into 2.5–4-cm/1–1½-inch pieces

2 teaspoons ground cumin

2 teaspoons ground coriander

½ teaspoon ground turmeric

½–¾ teaspoon cayenne pepper

salt

1 tablespoon lemon juice

3 tablespoons olive or rapeseed oil

½ teaspoon whole cumin seeds

1 medium onion, peeled and chopped

20 medium okra, about 140 g/5 oz, topped, tailed and cut in half

1 medium tomato, peeled (see page 267) and roughly chopped

Put the chicken in a non-reactive (ceramic, glass or stainless steel) bowl. Add the cumin, coriander, turmeric, cayenne pepper, 1 teaspoon salt and the lemon juice. Stir well. Cover and refrigerate for 1–2 hours.

Put the oil in a frying pan, preferably non-stick, and set it over a medium–high heat. When hot, put in the cumin seeds, onions and okra. Stir and fry for 6–7 minutes, or until the onions have browned a bit.

Add all the marinated chicken to the pan. Stir and fry for 3–4 minutes, or until the chicken pieces become opaque. (Do not worry if some of the spices stick to the pan.) Add 120 ml/4 fl oz water, ¼ teaspoon salt and the tomato. Stir and bring to a simmer. Cover, lower the heat and simmer gently for 10 minutes.

Tandoori-style Chicken with Mint

An 8–24-hour marination period is required here. This chicken tastes just as good hot as it does cold, making it perfect for everyday meals, formal dinners and picnics. Once cooked, if properly wrapped and refrigerated, the chicken will keep for a good 5–6 days   **Serves 4**

4 whole chicken legs (about 1.25 kg/2¾ lb), skinned and separated into drumsticks and thighs

1 teaspoon salt

2 tablespoons lemon juice

½ medium onion, peeled and chopped

3 cloves garlic, peeled and chopped

7.5-cm/3-inch piece of fresh ginger, peeled and chopped

½ teaspoon cayenne pepper

1 teaspoon garam masala, home-made (see page 264) or shop-bought

2 teaspoons ground cumin

250 ml/8 fl oz natural yoghurt

3 tablespoons olive or rapeseed oil or ghee

4 tablespoons finely chopped fresh mint

Cut 2 deep diagonal slits into the fleshy parts of each thigh and each drumstick. Put the chicken pieces on a large plate in a single layer. Rub both sides first with the salt and then the lemon juice. Set aside for 20 minutes.

Meanwhile, put the onion, garlic, ginger, cayenne pepper, garam masala, cumin and yoghurt into a blender and blend until you have a smooth paste. Put the chicken and all the accumulated juices in a bowl. Add the paste from the blender and mix well. Cover and refrigerate overnight or for up to 24 hours.

Preheat the oven to 240°C/gas mark 9.

Remove the chicken from the marinade and lay the pieces in a single layer in a baking tin. Brush with oil and then sprinkle with half the mint. Bake for 15 minutes. Turn the pieces over, brush with more oil and sprinkle the remaining mint over the top. Bake for another 5 minutes or until the chicken is cooked.

Baked Chicken Curry

Here the chicken is marinated overnight with most of the ingredients, then baked in its marinating dish, magically creating a curry. If a slightly sweet taste is desired, two tablespoons of sultanas may be added to the marinade. Serve with rice and Green Lentils with Green Beans & Fresh Coriander (see page 195) **Serves 4**

1.25 kg/2¾ lb bone-in chicken pieces

1 teaspoon salt

freshly ground black pepper

2 tablespoons lemon juice

2 teaspoons peeled and finely grated fresh ginger

1 large clove garlic, peeled and crushed

5 tablespoons full-fat, natural yoghurt

1½ tablespoons ground coriander

2 teaspoons ground cumin

½ teaspoon ground turmeric

½ teaspoon cayenne pepper

6 cardamom pods

oil, for basting

2 tablespoons peeled and finely chopped red onion or shallot

Put the chicken in a large casserole dish in a single layer. Add the salt, lots of black pepper and the lemon juice. Mix well and set aside for 20 minutes.

Combine the ginger, garlic, yoghurt, coriander, cumin, turmeric, cayenne pepper and cardamom in a bowl. Mix well. Rub the chicken with this mixture, then cover and refrigerate overnight.

Preheat the oven to 200°C/gas mark 6.

Bring the chicken to room temperature. Brush the top with oil and scatter the onions over the top. Place in the middle of the oven for 30 minutes. Turn the chicken pieces over and put back in the oven. Cook for another 40 minutes, basting every 10 minutes with the juices.

Chicken Roasted with Ginger & Coriander

There is something about the combination of fresh ginger and fresh coriander that tastes very Indian, very Delhi, to me, very much like home. In India, where few people have ovens, the chicken is browned first with the spices in a pan and then cooked on the hob over a low flame. I have, over the years, mastered making it in the oven only because it requires much less effort and the results are exactly the same. This chicken may be served hot, with rice or breads (pita bread is fine too), a green vegetable and Black Beans (see page 182) served on the side, but it is also excellent when cold, and perfect for picnics **Serves 4–5**

1.5 kg/3 lb 3 oz chicken legs (about 5), separated into drumsticks and thighs

1½ teaspoons salt

freshly ground black pepper

½ teaspoon cayenne pepper, or to taste

1 teaspoon garam masala, home-made (see page 264) or shop-bought

1 teaspoon peeled and finely grated fresh ginger

2 tablespoons natural yoghurt, preferably a 'bio' variety

60 g/2 oz chopped fresh coriander (do not use the coarser stems)

Preheat the oven to 200°C/gas mark 6.

Lay the chicken pieces in a single layer in a lasagne-type baking dish. Sprinkle the salt, pepper, cayenne pepper and garam masala evenly on all sides and pat in. Now rub the ginger, yoghurt and coriander all over the pieces, leaving them skin side down. Place the baking dish in the oven and bake for 25 minutes. Turn the chicken pieces over. Continue to bake, basting with the pan juices every 10 minutes, until the chicken is cooked through and the tops have browned, another 35 minutes.

Chicken with Spinach

Here, again, is one of my party favourites as it is quite easy to prepare and may be done ahead of time and reheated. I do all the chopping in a food processor, which takes just a few minutes, but you may do it by hand if you prefer: the results will be the same. While I have used fresh spinach only because I grow so much of it, frozen, chopped spinach may be used instead. For a dinner, I might serve this with Rice Pilaf with Almonds & Sultanas and Aubergines in a North-south Sauce (see pages 203 and 144) plus a yoghurt relish **Serves 6**

6 chicken legs, separated into drumsticks and thighs, or any other chicken parts you like (about 1.9 kg/4¼ lb in total)

salt and freshly ground black pepper

2 medium onions, peeled and coarsely chopped

5-cm/2-inch piece of fresh ginger, peeled and roughly chopped

6 medium cloves garlic, peeled and coarsely chopped

1 tablespoon sweet red paprika

½ teaspoon cayenne pepper

5 tablespoons olive or rapeseed oil

2 x 5-cm/2-inch cinnamon sticks

8 cardamom pods

285 g/10 oz spinach, chopped (defrosted and lightly drained if frozen)

Spread the chicken out in a single layer and sprinkle 1 teaspoon salt and lots of black pepper on all sides.

Put the onions, ginger, garlic, paprika and cayenne pepper into a food processor and, using a fast start-and-stop method, chop all the ingredients as finely as possible, stopping short of making a purée.

Put the oil into a wide, heavy pan (a large non-stick sauté pan or well-seasoned wok is ideal) and set over a medium–high heat. When hot, put in the cinnamon and cardamom. Let them sizzle for a few seconds. Now put in as much chicken as will fit easily in a single layer, and brown on all sides. Transfer to a bowl, leaving the whole spices behind. Brown all the chicken in this way and keep in the bowl.

Put the onion mixture into the pan, reducing the heat to medium. Stir and fry for 4–5 minutes, until most of the liquid has evaporated. Add the spinach and ½ teaspoon salt. Stir and fry another 4–5 minutes.

Add the chicken, ¼ teaspoon salt and 120 ml/4 fl oz water. Bring to the boil. Cover, lower the heat and simmer gently for 25 minutes, gently turning the chicken pieces a few times. Excess fat may be removed before serving.

Chicken with Apricots

The Parsi community of India is of Persian descent. When the Parsis fled Iran in the 10th century, they settled on India's west coast, where they managed to preserve not only their religious traditions – they are Zoroastrians – but many of their culinary traditions as well. This delicately sweet-and-sour dish of chicken cooked with dried apricots is one of them. However, Parsis gradually picked up customs from their Gujarati neighbours, and their 19th-century colonial masters, the British, in Bombay. I have a Parsi friend who puts in a healthy glug of Madeira towards the end of the cooking. This dish is generally served with a mountain of very fine, crisp potato straws but it may also be served with rice **Serves 4**

1.25 kg/2½ lb chicken pieces (I use 8 thighs or drumsticks, or a mixture of the two, but a cut-up chicken would be fine)

salt and freshly ground black pepper

12 dried apricots, preferably the orange Turkish ones

3 tablespoons olive or rapeseed oil

2 cinnamon sticks

½ teaspoon whole cumin seeds

2 medium onions, peeled and cut into fine half-rings

3 teaspoons peeled and finely grated fresh ginger

1 tablespoon tomato purée

1½ tablespoons granulated sugar

2 tablespoons red wine vinegar

1 teaspoon garam masala, preferably home-made (see page 264), but shop-bought will do

½–¾ teaspoon cayenne pepper

Sprinkle the chicken on all sides with ½ teaspoon salt and generous amounts of black pepper. Pat in and set aside.

Put the apricots in a small pan with 250 ml/8 fl oz water and bring to the boil. Lower the heat and gently simmer for 15 minutes, or until the apricots have softened but are firm enough to be cooked again later. Leave in their liquid.

Put the oil in a large frying pan or sauté pan and set over a medium–high heat. When hot, put in the cinnamon sticks and cumin. Ten seconds later, put in half the chicken pieces and brown them on all sides. Transfer to a bowl. Cook the remaining chicken in the same way. Add to the bowl.

Add the onions to the pan. Stir and fry until they brown at the edges. Add the ginger and stir for a few seconds. Add the tomato purée and stir once. Now return the chicken and all the accumulated juices to the pan, along with 350 ml/12 fl oz water and 1 teaspoon salt. Cover and bring to the boil. Lower the heat and cook gently for 15 minutes, turning the chicken once during this time.

Remove the cover and add the sugar, vinegar, apricots and their cooking liquid, garam masala and cayenne pepper. Stir and cook over a high heat until the sauce is a bit syrupy.

Chicken Baked in a Packet

You could use any chicken parts you like for this recipe – dark meat, light meat, or a combination. The bones should stay in, but the skin should be removed. This chicken needs to be marinated for at least four hours. Serve with Plain Basmati Rice, My Everyday Moong Dal and Spinach with Garlic & Cumin (see pages 201, 192 and 169), plus a yoghurt relish and a salad to get the feel of a simple family meal in northern India   **Serves 2–4**

1 teaspoon ground coriander

1 teaspoon ground cumin

2 teaspoons sweet red paprika

¼–½ teaspoon cayenne pepper

½ teaspoon ground turmeric

2 cloves garlic, peeled and crushed

1½ teaspoons peeled and finely grated fresh ginger

3 tablespoons full-fat natural yoghurt

2 teaspoons lemon juice

1 teaspoon salt

freshly ground black pepper

675 g/1½ lb bone-in chicken pieces, skinned

Combine all the ingredients apart from the chicken in a non-reactive (ceramic, glass or stainless steel) bowl. Mix to make a paste.

Place a 60-cm/24-inch piece of foil in front of you. Cut deep slits on the fleshy sides of the meat pieces, staying away from the edges. Lay the pieces side by side in a single row in the centre of the foil. Rub the spice paste all over them, going deep into the slits. Fold the top of the foil over the chicken, then the bottom and finally the two sides. Refrigerate the packet for at least 4 hours, or overnight.

Preheat the oven to 200°C/gas mark 6.

Place the chicken packet in a baking tin and bake for 30 minutes. Open the packet carefully and turn the chicken pieces over, basting with the juices. Close the packet again and bake for another 15 minutes.

Bangladeshi White Chicken Korma

I had this dish in Bangladesh and thought it was exquisite. It seemed to have come straight from the palaces of 17th-century Moghul rulers. It was a true korma, mildly but beautifully seasoned, and without any brown, yellow or red spices to mar its pallor. There were some New World sliced green chillies scattered over the top. Of course, it helps to get a good-quality organic chicken. Ask your butcher to skin it and cut it into small serving pieces (each breast into six, each leg into two, wings into three, back into three, neck into two). Serve this with rice or flatbreads, or even in a Western way with potatoes and a vegetable. **Serves 4**

4 tablespoons olive or rapeseed oil, or ghee

3 x 5-cm/2-inch cinnamon sticks

3 bay leaves

10 cardamom pods

1 medium onion, peeled and sliced into fine half-rings

1 x 1.6-kg/3¾-lb chicken, skinned and cut into small serving pieces (as described above)

½ medium onion, peeled and very finely chopped

3 tablespoons peeled and finely grated fresh ginger

6 cloves garlic, peeled and crushed

120 ml/4 fl oz 'bio' yoghurt, or ordinary natural yoghurt + 1 tablespoon lemon juice, beaten until smooth

1¼ teaspoons salt

1–2 teaspoons finely chopped fresh, hot green chillies

Put the oil into a large, deep frying pan or sauté pan and set over a medium–high heat. When the oil is really hot, put in the cinnamon, bay leaves and cardamom. Stir for 10 seconds as the spices sizzle. Add the sliced onions. Stir and fry for about 3 minutes or until they brown a bit. Add the chicken pieces. Stir and cook for 5–6 minutes, or until they are lightly browned.

Add the chopped onion, the ginger and garlic. Stir and fry for 2 minutes. Add the yoghurt and salt. Stir and cook for 10 minutes.

Add the chillies and 3 tablespoons water. Bring to a simmer. Cover, lower the heat and simmer very gently for another 10–15 minutes, or until the chicken is tender.

Kerala-style Chicken Curry

Here is a creamy, coconut–enriched chicken curry that takes me back to the balmy south-west breezes of Kerala's palm-lined coast. Serve with Plain Jasmine Rice (see page 211) and a vegetable **Serves 4**

3 tablespoons olive or rapeseed oil

½ teaspoon whole cumin seeds

½ teaspoon whole brown mustard seeds

1 medium onion, peeled and sliced into fine half-rings

2 teaspoons peeled and finely grated fresh ginger

4 cloves garlic, peeled and finely chopped

1.25 kg/2¾ lb chicken pieces, skinned

½ teaspoon cayenne pepper (or more, if desired)

1 tablespoon sweet red paprika

1 teaspoon salt

15–20 fresh curry leaves, if available, or 8 fresh basil leaves, torn

250 ml/8 fl oz coconut milk, from a well-shaken can

Put the oil into a wide pan and set over a medium–high heat. When hot, put in the cumin and mustard seeds. As soon as the mustard seeds begin to pop, a matter of seconds, add the onions. Stir and fry until they have browned lightly. Add the ginger, garlic, chicken, cayenne pepper, paprika, salt and curry leaves. Stir for a minute. Add 250 ml/8 fl oz water and bring to a simmer. Cover, lower the heat and simmer gently for 25 minutes, stirring now and then.

Remove the lid and boil down most of the liquid. Add the coconut milk and cook, stirring over a medium–high heat, for 1 minute.

Chicken with Vindaloo Spices

'Vindaloo' implies garlic and vinegar, and this dish certainly has plenty of both. Make it as hot as you like. The heat balances the tartness. The dish keeps well and, because it does not have too much sauce, is wonderful to take on picnics **Serves 4**

4 tablespoons olive or rapeseed oil

½ teaspoon whole brown mustard seeds

¼ teaspoon whole fenugreek seeds

1 teaspoon whole black peppercorns

15–20 fresh curry leaves or 10 fresh basil leaves, torn

8 chicken thighs

6 cloves garlic, peeled and chopped

250 ml/8 fl oz cider vinegar or white wine vinegar

1¼ teaspoons salt

1½ teaspoons ground cumin

1 tablespoon ground coriander

½–1 teaspoon cayenne pepper (more if you wish)

1 tablespoon sweet red paprika

Put the oil in a large sauté pan or wide frying pan – anything large enough to hold the chicken in a single layer. Set over a medium–high heat. When hot, put in the mustard seeds. As soon as they pop, a matter of seconds, put in the fenugreek seeds and peppercorns. A few seconds later put in the curry leaves, chicken and all the remaining ingredients. Stir and bring to the boil. Cover, lower the heat and simmer gently for 20 minutes.

Remove the cover, turn the heat to high and cook, stirring and turning, until all the liquid evaporates and the chicken browns on all sides.

Chicken Curry with Cardamom

A gentle, family-style curry. If you leave out the cayenne pepper, this may even be served to small children. Serve with rice and perhaps Corn with Aromatic Seasonings (see page 149)

Serves 4

5 tablespoons olive or rapeseed oil

2 x 5-cm/2-inch cinnamon sticks

8 cardamom pods

1 x 1.6-kg/3¾-lb chicken, cut into 10–12 serving pieces

2 medium onions, peeled and chopped

2 cloves garlic, peeled and finely chopped

2 tablespoons ground coriander

1 tablespoon ground cumin

¼ teaspoon ground turmeric

½ teaspoon cayenne pepper, or to taste

2 medium tomatoes, chopped

1 litre/32 fl oz chicken stock

salt

Put the oil in a large, wide sauté pan over a high heat. When hot, put in the cinnamon and cardamom. Ten seconds later, put in as many chicken pieces as will fit easily and brown them until golden on all sides. Transfer to a bowl, leaving the whole spices in the pan. Brown the remaining chicken in the same way and add to the bowl.

Add the onions to the pan, reducing the heat to medium and sauté until they start to brown lightly at the edges. Add the garlic and stir a few times. Now add the coriander, cumin, turmeric and cayenne pepper. Stir once or twice. Put in the tomatoes, stirring until they begin to soften.

Return the browned chicken and all its accumulated juices to the pan, along with the chicken stock, ½ teaspoon salt if the stock is salted, 1 teaspoon if not, and bring to the boil. Cover and cook somewhat rapidly over a medium heat for 15 minutes.

Remove the cover and turn the heat to high. Cook, stirring now and then until the sauce has thickened.

Whole Chicken Baked with an Almond & Onion

Sauce This is an oven-cooked version of the Indian classic *murgh mussallam* – a whole chicken cooked in a rich, spicy sauce. Indians like their chicken skinned, partly to let the spices penetrate better. I have not bothered too much with that in this book, to make life easier, but it would be helpful to do it here as this is a dish for special occasions. You can ask your butcher to skin the chicken but it is not difficult to do yourself. The wings are a bit troublesome, so I just leave them alone. I might go to town here, serving Black Beans, Yellow Basmati Rice with Sesame Seeds, and Sweet & Sour Aubergines (see pages 182, 202 and 142). On the other hand, you could serve it as a spicy roast. **Serves 4**

1 x 1.6-kg/3¾-lb chicken

½ teaspoon salt

1 tablespoon lemon juice

3 tablespoons olive or
  rapeseed oil

½ teaspoon whole cumin seeds

For the spice paste

2 tablespoons lemon juice

250 ml/8 fl oz natural yoghurt

1 medium onion, peeled and
  chopped

7.5-cm/3-inch piece of fresh
  ginger, peeled and chopped

3 large cloves garlic, peeled
  and chopped

¾ teaspoon cayenne pepper

1¾ teaspoons salt

2 teaspoons garam masala,
  preferably home-made (see
  page 264), but shop-bought
  will do

2 tablespoons blanched,
  slivered almonds

Combine all the spice paste ingredients in a blender in the order listed. Blend to a smooth paste.

Remove as much of the chicken skin as you can. Cut 2–3 deep, diagonal gashes in the fleshy part of each breast and thigh. Rub ½ teaspoon salt and 1 tablespoon lemon juice all over the chicken, inside and out. Leave for 15 minutes. Now put the chicken in a bowl. Spread the spice paste all over, then cover and refrigerate for 4–24 hours.

Preheat the oven to 200°C/gas mark 6.

Put the oil in a large, flameproof casserole large enough to enclose the chicken and set over a medium–high heat. When hot, put in the cumin seeds. Let them sizzle for 10 seconds, then put in the whole chicken, breast up, as well as all the spice paste. Bring to a simmer. Cover and place in the oven. Bake for 30 minutes. Remove the lid and bake uncovered for another 40 minutes or so, basting with the sauce every 10 minutes, until the chicken is tender.

Turkey Chappali Kebabs

Chappali kebabs, popular throughout much of Pakistan but originating near its borders with Afghanistan, are actually beef patties (rather than skewered meat) shallow-fried in the fat rendered from the tail of a fat-tailed sheep. If you can imagine a juicy, spicy hamburger cooked in roast beef dripping, you get the general idea: delicious but iffy on the health front. Over the years, I have come up with my own version, using turkey meat.

I serve these kebabs with Thin Raw Onion Rings and Peshawari Red Pepper Chutney (see pages 236 and 238). You may even put this kebab in a hamburger bun, along with the onion rings and either a good squirt of lemon juice or some tomato ketchup **Makes 6 kebabs**

---

2 tablespoons natural yoghurt

450 g/1 lb minced turkey, preferably a mixture of light and dark meat

¾ teaspoon salt, or to taste

1 tablespoon whole coriander seeds and 1 teaspoon whole cumin seeds, lightly crushed in a mortar, or put between sheets of foil and crushed with a rolling pin

4 tablespoons finely chopped fresh mint

½ teaspoon crushed red chilli flakes

1 teaspoon peeled and finely grated fresh ginger

5 tablespoons olive or rapeseed oil

Put the yoghurt in a small sieve and set it over a cup as you prepare the rest of your ingredients (10 minutes will do, but longer will not hurt).

Put the strained yoghurt and all the remaining ingredients except the oil in a bowl. Mix well. Cover and refrigerate for at least 1 hour, or as long as 24 hours, so that the flavours mingle.

Divide the meat into six pieces and roll into balls. Flatten the balls to make six clean-edged patties 9 cm/3½ inches.

Put the oil in a large frying pan and set over a medium–high heat. When hot, put in as many patties as will fit easily and fry for about 1 minute on each side, or until browned. Turn the heat down to medium–low and continue to cook the patties, turning frequently, until the juices run clear when the patties are pressed. Cook all the patties in this way and serve hot.

Minced Turkey with Hyderabadi Seasonings

Known as a keema (minced meat), this dish can also be made with minced lamb or, for that matter, with minced beef. When using turkey, make sure your butcher includes both light and dark meat, as white meat alone will be very dry. In Hyderabad this is typically served at Sunday brunches with khichri (the dish of rice and split peas from which the British kedgeree was derived, see page 209), poppadoms for crunch, pickles for pizzazz and a yoghurt relish. Shop-bought Indian pickles, such as mango, lemon or chilli, will do, but if you prefer, a sweeter shop-bought chutney would be just fine **Serves 4**

3 tablespoons olive or rapeseed oil

1 teaspoon whole mustard seeds

1 teaspoon whole cumin seeds

2 dried, hot red chillies

10 fresh curry leaves or 5 fresh basil leaves, crushed/torn

60 g/2 oz peeled and finely chopped onion

2 cloves garlic, peeled and crushed

2 teaspoons peeled and finely grated fresh ginger

450 g/1 lb minced turkey, dark and light meat combined

1 tablespoon ground coriander

1 teaspoon ground cumin

4 tablespoons natural yoghurt

150 g/5½ oz peas, defrosted if frozen

1 teaspoon salt

Put the oil in a frying pan and set over a medium–high heat. When hot, put in the mustard seeds, the cumin seeds and the chillies. As soon as the mustard seeds begin to pop, a matter of seconds, add the curry leaves and the onion. Stir and fry until the onion pieces turn brown at the edges. Add the garlic and ginger. Stir for 30 seconds.

Add the minced turkey to the pan. Lower the heat to medium. Stir as you break up all the lumps in the meat. Add the coriander, cumin, yoghurt and 120 ml/4 fl oz water. Stir and bring to the boil. Cover, lower the heat and cook for 35 minutes. Add the peas, salt and 50 ml/2 fl oz water. Stir, then cover and cook for another 7–10 minutes.

Tandoori-style Duck Breasts

These duck breasts are not cooked in a tandoor, or even in an oven, but they do taste like tandoor-baked poultry, hence their name. I marinate them in the same manner that I would a tandoori chicken, then I quickly pan-fry them so that they stay a little rare inside. They take just minutes to cook. As for the skin, which is flabby if not crisped to perfection, I just remove it entirely. Serve with Sri Lankan Rice with Fresh Coriander and Lemon Grass and Swiss Chard with Ginger and Garlic (see pages 205 and 148) **Serves 4**

For the marinade

1 tablespoon lemon juice

2 tablespoons natural yoghurt

½ medium onion, peeled and chopped

2 cloves garlic, peeled and chopped

5-cm/2-inch piece of fresh ginger, peeled and chopped

¼ teaspoon cayenne pepper

1¼ teaspoons salt

½ teaspoon ground turmeric

1 teaspoon garam masala, preferably home-made (see page 264), but shop-bought will do

To cook the duck

4 duck breasts (about 900 g/ 2 lb in total)

1 tablespoon olive or rapeseed oil

Put the marinade ingredients in a blender in the order listed and blend until smooth.

Remove the duck skin. Pat the breasts with kitchen paper until dry. Rub the marinade on both sides of each breast and put in a non-reactive (ceramic, glass or stainless steel) bowl. Cover and refrigerate for at least 6 hours, or overnight.

Pick up one breast. Most of the marinade will drop off, but some will still cling to the meat: that is all you want. Put the breast flat on a board and cut it crossways, holding the knife at a slight diagonal, into slices 7mm/⅓ inch thick. Cut all the duck pieces in this way.

Just before eating, set a large, heavy frying pan (preferably cast iron) over a medium–high heat. Let it get very hot. Brush it with oil. Now lay about 8 slices of duck in the hot pan. As soon as they are lightly browned, a matter of seconds, turn them over and quickly brown the second side. Transfer to a warm plate and cover loosely. Cook all the slices in this way and serve hot.

Pakistani Bhuna Quail

South Asians love their quail, which is generally brought home by hunters. I know that when the men in our family returned from their winter shoots, what I most looked forward to eating were not the deer and geese, but the smaller creatures – the duck, partridge and quail. Here is a quick, stir-fried version of a dish I had in Lahore, Pakistan ('bhuna' implies stirring and browning). This recipe may be easily doubled, but use a very large frying pan if you do so.

When eating quail you have to use your fingers. It is hard to focus on any other food, even though rice, vegetables, other meats and legumes are nearly always part of the meal   **Serves 2**

1 medium tomato, chopped

1 large clove garlic, peeled and chopped

1-cm/½-inch piece of fresh ginger, peeled and chopped

1 medium shallot, peeled and chopped

¾ teaspoon salt

½ teaspoon garam masala, preferably home-made (see page 264), but shop-bought will do

¼ teaspoon cayenne pepper

¼ teaspoon ground turmeric

2 quail, split lengthways

2 tablespoons olive or rapeseed oil

4 cardamom pods

Put the tomato, garlic, ginger, shallot, salt, garam masala, cayenne pepper and turmeric in a blender and blend until smooth. Pour into a bowl. Add the quail. Mix well, then cover and leave to marinate for 2–4 hours in the refrigerator.

Put the oil in a frying pan and set over a medium–high heat. When hot, put in the cardamom pods. Ten seconds later empty the contents of the bowl into the frying pan and bring to the boil. Cover, lower the heat to medium and cook for about 10 minutes, or until most of the liquid has evaporated. Remove the cover. Now stir and brown the spice paste and quail, sprinkling the pan with water every time the spices seem to be catching. Keep doing so for about 5 minutes. By this time the quail should be lightly browned and cooked through, and the spices, also browned, should form a thick paste around them.

Lamb, Goat, Pork & Beef

Contrary to what many people in the West assume, a good 70 per cent of Indians eat meat. They may not be able to afford it every day, or to buy it for lunch *and* dinner, but they eat it all the same and with relish.

Several methods of cooking it have come down from ancient times, when game was roasted on skewers and spits, pork was slowly braised in barely bubbling pots, beef was stir-fried in wok-like *karhais* with aromatic spices, lamb was cooked in packets of banana leaves, and goat was gently stewed – in coconut milk in the south, and in cow's milk in northern Kashmir.

Indians have adapted most of these methods to newer appliances, such as electric hobs and grills, which are quite common in middle-class and upper-class homes (and that means more than 300 million people). But there are diehards, who although wealthy enough to afford simple hobs, insist that Indian foods taste best when cooked over wood, so some old traditions still survive. I know a few of these diehards; most have a servant who does the cooking and the scrubbing of the blackened pots!

This chapter contains a range of dishes, from grilled meats to braised pot-roasts. To make each of them successfully, the cut of meat is important.

Meat for Curries

In India and its neighbouring countries, most curries are made with unboned goat meat. Shoppers generally choose a bit of neck, a bit of shoulder and a bit of shank meat and marrow bone, sometimes a bit of rib as well. The bones give a depth of flavour to the sauce. Most Westerners cannot deal with bones, and goat is harder to find anyway, so is not a common choice. Consequently, I have used boneless lamb for most of my recipes, and the options are outlined below.

Lamb I like the texture of shoulder meat, which is moister than leg. Ask the butcher to cut it into boneless cubes measuring about 2.5–4 cm/1–1½ inches. Save the bones for soups and stock, and freeze the meat you do not want to cook immediately in convenient amounts.

Goat Goat meat is now increasingly available, being sold at *halal*, West Indian and specialist butchers. For curries, you need some pieces of meat with bone and some without. The pieces should, ideally, come from different parts of the animal – the shoulder, upper leg and shank, plus a few from the neck – and should be cut into 4-cm/1-inch cubes. Unboned pieces could be larger. I always like to include at least one marrow bone.

Pork It is mostly the Christians of southern Asia who love pork, though very often Hindus will eat it too. In the formerly Portuguese colony of Goa, every part of the pig is eaten, from ears to tails. Use the parts my recipes suggest – no ears and tails, promise!

Beef Hindus in India do not generally eat beef (it was not cooked in our Delhi kitchen, though we were free to eat it outside the home in hotels and restaurants), but Christians and Muslims in India, Pakistan, Bangladesh and Sri Lanka certainly do cook it frequently. Use the cuts my recipes suggest.

Kebabs South Asians, especially those of the meat-eating fraternity, love their kebabs. This is especially true in my community, where we were always known as *sharabi-kebabis* (drinkers and eaters), 'kebab' here standing for all good food. Kebabs are the ideal accompaniment to drinks, are easy first courses (at Kashmiri banquets they sit atop hillocks of basmati rice at the very start of the meal), and in countries such as Pakistan can have whole meals built around them.

They can be made out of cubed meat or minced meat. They may be cooked on skewers or slapped on to hot stones or griddles, or even baked. In Bangladesh leftover minced meat kebabs are crumbled into the next day's dal (split peas) to give it a special flavour.

Even though India has an ancient history of both roasted and grilled meats, kebabs, and even the word itself, owe their origins to the Arab world where the simplest kebabs were cubes of lamb marinated in olive oil and garlic, skewered and then grilled. When Muslim invaders from the north first came into India in the 10th and 11th centuries, they brought the concept of kebabs with them. But India had no olive oil. All we had was mustard oil, which has a strong flavour and aroma. We can only deduce that they must have substituted one for the other, as many kebab dishes in Pakistan and northern India have a touch of mustard oil in them.

Punjabi Lamb Kebabs

This is a basic Indian kebab recipe that has probably not changed much since the 16th century, except for the addition of chillies and what is now the ubiquitous chaat masala, a mixture of spices that most Indians buy in the market. It adds a spicy sourness. If you can't find it, sprinkle a dash of cayenne and roasted ground cumin seeds over the kebabs and add squirts of lime juice. Mustard oil is interesting. I have seen it used for kebabs in India and Pakistan. Both countries have a Punjab, as that state, today on India's western border and Pakistan's eastern border, was split in two when the British partitioned India. I like to have these kebabs with Rice Pilaf with Almonds & Sultanas and Sweet & Sour Aubergines (see pages 203 and 142) **Serves 4–6**

175 ml/6 fl oz full-fat yoghurt, preferably Greek

6 tablespoons mustard oil or extra virgin olive oil

1¼ teaspoons salt

1 teaspoon cayenne pepper

2 cloves garlic, peeled and crushed

2 teaspoons peeled and finely grated fresh ginger (see page 265)

2 teaspoons garam masala (shop-bought is fine)

1.25 kg/2½ lb boneless lamb from the leg, cut into 2.5-cm/1-inch cubes

3 tablespoons melted butter

1 teaspoon chaat masala, or see suggestion above

Put the yoghurt in a cloth-lined colander set in the sink. Leave for 10–15 minutes. Put the drained yoghurt in a bowl. Add the oil, salt, cayenne pepper, garlic, ginger and garam masala and beat well with a whisk. Add the meat and mix again. Cover and refrigerate overnight, or for as long as 24 hours.

Preheat the grill to its highest setting.

Push 4 skewers through the centre of the lamb cubes, dividing the meat equally and leaving the marinade behind. Brush generously with the melted butter. Rest the two ends of each skewer on the rim of the grill pan so that the kebabs are suspended and the pan catches the drips. Place the pan about 13 cm/5 inches from the source of heat. Grill for 5–7 minutes on one side, then 5–7 minutes on the opposite side, or until the kebabs are done to your liking. Sprinkle the chaat masala over the top.

Lamb Kebabs with Mint

While these kebabs, freshly grilled and hot, are always popular at mealtimes, they are also loved outdoors on picnics. In fact, if properly wrapped and refrigerated after cooking, they will keep for a good 5–6 days, making them perfect for an impromptu cold meal. For a hot meal, serve with a rice dish and Indian vegetables. For a picnic, serve with salads and crusty French bread **Serves 4–6**

6 tablespoons natural yoghurt

1 tablespoon lemon juice

1¼ teaspoons salt

½ teaspoon cayenne pepper

2 teaspoons ground cumin

2 teaspoons ground coriander

½ medium onion, peeled and chopped

2.5-cm/1-inch piece of fresh ginger, peeled and chopped

1.25 kg/2½ lb boneless lamb cubes, cut from the leg

3–4 tablespoons finely chopped fresh mint

oil, for brushing

Combine the yoghurt, lemon juice, salt, cayenne pepper, cumin, coriander, onion and ginger in a blender. Blend until you have a smooth paste.

Put the lamb in a non-reactive (ceramic, glass or stainless steel) bowl and pour the paste from the blender over the top. Mix well and prod the lamb cubes with a fork. Cover and refrigerate overnight, or for as long as 24 hours.

Preheat the grill to its highest setting.

Push 4 skewers through the centre of the lamb cubes, dividing the meat equally and leaving the marinade behind. Sprinkle mint all over the kebabs and brush with the oil. Rest the two ends of each skewer on the rim of the grill pan so that the kebabs are suspended and the pan catches the drips. Place the pan about 13 cm/5 inches from the source of heat. Grill for 5–7 minutes on one side, then 5–7 minutes on the opposite side, or until the kebabs are done to your liking.

Delhi-style Bhuna Lamb

Bhuna means 'browned', actually the process of browning, so in this dish the meat has a browned look to it, and the sauce is thick and clings to the meat. This is a family recipe that comes via my niece Abha. If you like, add two slit, hot green chillies at the same time as the green coriander, just before the final stir. I like to eat this with Indian flatbreads (pita or other shop-bought flatbreads may be substituted) as well as Potato & Pea Curry (see page 167). You could also serve it with rice **Serves 4–6**

5 tablespoons olive or rapeseed oil

1 cinnamon stick

2 bay leaves

8 cardamom pods

180 g/6 oz peeled and finely chopped onions

2 large cloves garlic, peeled and crushed

4-cm/1½-inch piece of fresh ginger, peeled and finely grated

900 g/2 lb boneless lamb from the shoulder, cut into 3-cm/1¼-inch pieces

½ teaspoon cayenne pepper

1¼–1½ teaspoons salt

1 teaspoon garam masala, home-made (see page 264) or shop-bought

4 tablespoons finely chopped fresh coriander

Put the oil in a wide, heavy pan and set over a medium–high heat. When hot, put in the cinnamon, bay leaves and cardamom. Let these sizzle for 10 seconds. Now put in the onions. Stir and fry until they start to turn brown at the edges. Add the garlic and ginger. Stir once or twice.

Now add the meat. Stir until it loses its raw colour. Add the cayenne pepper, salt and 350 ml/12 fl oz water. Stir and bring to the boil. Cover tightly, turn heat to low and cook for 60–70 minutes, or until the meat is tender. Remove the lid and turn the heat to high. Stir and cook until most of the liquid has been absorbed and the meat has a brownish (bhuna) look. Add the garam masala and coriander. Stir to mix and turn off the heat.

Lemony Minced Lamb with Mint & Coriander

You need a fair amount of the fresh mint and coriander here so that the meat really tastes both lemony and herbal. The ginger adds to the fresh, cleansing feeling. Serve with flatbreads or rice. For a snack, this minced meat, or keema, may be rolled up in flatbread along with finely sliced shallots, chopped tomatoes and, if you like, chopped fresh green chillies. In the Western world today this would be called a 'wrap'. As children we wrapped this keema in a chapati (a wholemeal flatbread) and my mother called it a *batta* **Serves 3–4**

2 tablespoons olive or rapeseed oil

2 x 5-cm/2-inch cinnamon sticks

4 tablespoons peeled and chopped onion

450 g/1 lb minced lamb (not too fatty)

2 teaspoons peeled and very finely grated fresh ginger

¾ teaspoon salt

½ teaspoon cayenne pepper, or to taste

4 tablespoons finely chopped fresh mint, leaves only

4 tablespoons finely chopped fresh coriander, leaves only

2 tablespoons lemon juice

¾ teaspoon garam masala, home-made (see page 264) or shop-bought

Put the oil in a large frying pan and set over a medium–high heat. When hot, put in the cinnamon sticks. Let them sizzle for a few seconds. Add the onion. Stir and fry until it browns at the edges. Now add the lamb and ginger. Stir and fry for about 5 minutes, breaking up the chunks of meat as you do so. Add 250 ml/8 fl oz water, the salt and cayenne pepper. Stir and bring to a simmer. Cover, lower the heat and simmer gently for 30–40 minutes or until the meat is tender.

Remove the lid. Add the mint, coriander, lemon juice and garam masala. Stir, then cook, uncovered, over a low heat for another 5 minutes, stirring now and then. Spoon out any excess fat before serving.

Minced Lamb with Potatoes

Our family eats this so frequently, along with a moong dal, rice, a yoghurt relish and pickles, that we consider it to be our 'soul food' meal. Nothing fancy here, only the homey and soothing **Serves 4–6**

3 tablespoons olive or rapeseed oil

2 x 7.5-cm/3-inch cinnamon sticks

1 medium onion, peeled and finely chopped

1 teaspoon peeled and finely grated fresh ginger

3 cloves garlic, peeled and finely chopped

900 g/2 lb minced lamb

3 tablespoons natural yoghurt

3 tablespoons tomato passata (see page 268)

1 teaspoon ground cumin

2 teaspoons ground coriander

¼ teaspoon cayenne pepper

¼ teaspoon ground turmeric

1¾ teaspoons salt

285 g/10 oz potatoes, peeled and cut into 2-cm/¾-inch cubes

Put the oil in a large frying pan or sauté pan and set over a medium–high heat. When hot, put in the cinnamon sticks. Let them sizzle for 5 seconds. Put in the onion. Stir and fry until it browns at the edges. Add the ginger and garlic. Stir for 1 minute. Add the lamb. Stir and fry, breaking up the lumps until the meat loses its redness. Add the yoghurt, tomato passata, cumin, coriander, cayenne pepper and turmeric. Stir for 1 minute. Add the salt, potatoes and 475 ml/16 fl oz water. Stir and bring to the boil. Cover, lower the heat and cook gently for 30 minutes.

Kashmiri Lamb Dumpukht

'Dumpukht' cookery was made popular in India by the Moghul courts, starting around the 16th century. Meat or rice dishes were semi-prepared, or else, in the case of meats, they were thoroughly marinated, and then put in a pot with a lid that was sealed shut with dough. The pot was placed on lightly smouldering embers, and some embers were also placed on top of the lid, thus forming a kind of slow-cooking oven. This cooking style is still popular in India, Pakistan and Bangladesh. This is a royal-style dish, rich with almonds and saffron that are native to Kashmir, yet it is quite light. The quantities can easily be doubled. For a festive meal, serve with Aubergines in a North-south Sesame or Peanut Sauce (see pages 144 –5) and a rice dish **Serves 3–4**

560 g/1¼ lb boneless lamb, preferably from the shoulder, cut into 2.5–4-cm/1–1½-inch cubes

250 ml/8 fl oz full-fat yoghurt, preferably Greek or 'bio', lightly beaten with a fork until smooth

1½ teaspoons garam masala, preferably home-made (see page 264)

¾ teaspoon cayenne pepper

1½ teaspoons salt

10 cardamom pods

¼ teaspoon peppercorns

½ teaspoon saffron threads, crumbled

2 bay leaves

1 tablespoon sultanas

20 whole almonds, preferably skinned

Combine all the ingredients except the almonds in a non-reactive (ceramic, glass or stainless steel) bowl. Prick the meat with the tip of a knife so that the marinade can penetrate well. Mix thoroughly, cover and refrigerate overnight, or up to 24 hours.

Put the almonds in a heatproof bowl. Pour over enough boiling water to cover them and leave to soak overnight, or up to 24 hours.

Preheat the oven to 160°C/gas mark 3.

Lift the almonds out of their soaking liquid and peel them if they are not already skinned. Combine the meat, its marinade and the almonds in a flameproof pan. Bring to a low simmer over a medium–low heat, stirring all the time so that the yoghurt does not curdle. Turn off the heat. Cover the pan first with foil, crimping it tightly, and then with its lid. Place in the oven for 60–75 minutes, testing after an hour to see if the meat is tender; if not, return to the oven for 15 minutes.

Pakistani-style Grilled Lamb Chops

When I was last in Pakistan there was a very successful grill house in Karachi serving a thousand people per night. Bar-B-Q Tonight, as it was called, offered all manner of meats grilled in a style that is a mixture of Afghan and Pakistani culinary traditions. I have adapted one of their goat meat recipes to lamb. You may use the smaller rib chops or the larger, steak-like shoulder chops. They will have bone, of course, so 900 g/2 lb will serve 2–3 people. This recipe may also be used for beef steaks. I love this with Tomato Pullao and Pan-grilled Courgettes (see pages 206 and 152) **Serves 2–3**

4 teaspoons peeled and very finely grated fresh ginger

2 teaspoons peeled and finely crushed garlic

1 tablespoon lemon juice

1¼ teaspoons salt

½–¾ teaspoon cayenne pepper

freshly ground black pepper

½ teaspoon garam masala, preferably home-made (see page 264), but shop-bought will do

900 g/2 lb lamb chops, shoulder or rib

2 tablespoons mustard, olive or rapeseed oil

Combine the ginger, garlic, lemon juice, salt, cayenne pepper, black pepper and garam masala in a shallow dish large enough to hold the chops. Mix well. Rub this marinade on both sides of the lamb chops. Cover and set aside in the refrigerator 4–24 hours.

Just before eating, preheat the grill to its highest setting and place a rack 10–13 cm/4–5 inches from the source of heat.

Put the chops, with any marinade that clings to them easily, in a baking tin, brush both sides with oil, and place under the grill. Grill for 3–4 minutes on each side, or until browned. If the chops are 2.5 cm/1 inch thick, this timing will ensure they are still pink inside, the way I like them. If you want them more done, put them in an oven preheated to 180°C/gas mark 4 for 5–10 minutes, depending upon the thickness of the chops and the doneness desired.

Lamb Curry with Whole Spices

This is a very popular dish in Delhi, where it is made with unboned cubes of goat meat. I generally make it with lamb. I like to serve this with Indian flatbreads, but shop-bought pita bread or tortillas would be good too. A vegetable and a legume should be included at dinner-time **Serves 4–6**

6 tablespoons olive or rapeseed oil

8 cardamom pods

2 x 5-cm/2-inch cinnamon sticks

8 whole cloves

1 teaspoon whole cumin seeds

1 teaspoon whole fennel seeds

115 g/4 oz peeled and finely chopped onions

900 g/2 lb boneless lamb from the shoulder, cut into 4-cm/1½-inch pieces

300 ml/10 fl oz natural yoghurt, lightly beaten

2 tablespoons ground coriander

2 teaspoons peeled and finely grated fresh ginger, or 1 teaspoon ground ginger

½–¾ teaspoon cayenne pepper

1½ teaspoons salt, or to taste

Preheat the oven to 180°C/gas mark 4.

Put the oil into a large, wide, flameproof pan and set over a medium–high heat. When hot, put in the cardamom, cinnamon, cloves, cumin and fennel seeds. Stir once, then put in the onions. Fry until they just begin to brown. Add the meat and all the remaining ingredients. Stir to mix and bring to a simmer. Cover first with foil, crimping the edges, and then with the lid. Place in the oven and bake for 1¼ hours, or until the meat is just tender, stirring now and then.

Uncover and cook for another 15–20 minutes, or until the meat is a bit more dried out and slightly browned. Stir now and then during this period.

Green Lamb Curry

Here is a most delicious curry from western India that may also be made with chicken. It requires a lot of fresh coriander. Buy a big bunch, or two if they are skimpy, aiming at about 190–215 g/6½–7 oz. Once you have trimmed it by cutting off the lower, non-leafy stems, washed and chopped it, you should end up with about 100 g/3½ oz. The quantities in this recipe can be easily doubled. This curry may be eaten with a rice dish or Indian flatbreads. Mushroom and Pea Curry (see page 158) could be served on the side **Serves 3–4**

2 tablespoons lemon juice

100 g/3½ oz chopped fresh coriander (see above)

2.5-cm/1-inch piece of fresh ginger, peeled and chopped

4 good-sized cloves garlic, peeled and chopped

3–4 fresh, hot green chillies (such as bird's eye), chopped

½ teaspoon ground turmeric

1½ teaspoons salt

3 tablespoons olive or rapeseed oil

½ teaspoon whole fennel seeds

1 medium onion, peeled and chopped

560 g/1¼ lb boneless lamb, preferably from the shoulder, cut into 2.5–4-cm/1–1½-inch cubes

120 ml/4 fl oz coconut milk, from a well-shaken can

Put the lemon juice, 120 ml/4 fl oz water, the coriander, ginger, garlic, chillies, turmeric and salt, in this order, into a blender. Blend thoroughly, pushing down if necessary with a rubber spatula, until you have a fine paste.

Preheat the oven to 160°C/gas mark 3.

Put the oil in a flameproof casserole and set over a medium–high heat. When hot, put in the fennel seeds. Two seconds later, put in the onions. Stir and fry until they brown at the edges. Add the meat. Stir and fry over a high heat for 7–8 minutes, or until the meat is lightly browned.

Add the green sauce from the blender and bring to a simmer. Cover and place in the oven for 60–75 minutes, or until the meat is tender, checking after an hour. Take the casserole out of the oven, add the coconut milk and stir it in. Reheat gently just before serving.

Kerala Lamb Stew

Pronounced 'eshtew' by the locals, this aromatic, soul-satisfying stew is a much-loved dish, often eaten by the Syrian Christians of the south-western state of Kerala at Easter. It has all the spices that grow in the backyards of Kerala homes – cinnamon, cardamom, cloves and peppercorns. It also has the Kerala staple, coconut milk. While this dish is generally served with rice pancakes known as *appams* ('appam and stew' being a pairing somewhat akin to 'sausage and mash' or 'fish and chips'), rice also works well   **Serves 4**

4 tablespoons olive or rapeseed oil

2 x 7.5-cm/3-inch cinnamon sticks

½ teaspoon whole black peppercorns

10 cloves

10 cardamom pods

1 large red onion, peeled and finely chopped

20 or so fresh curry leaves or 10 fresh basil leaves, torn

2 teaspoons peeled and very finely grated fresh ginger

900 g/2 lb stewing lamb

450 g/1 lb boiling potatoes, peeled and diced into 2.5-cm/1-inch cubes

4 medium carrots, peeled and cut into 4-cm/1½-inch chunks

1¾ teaspoons salt

¼–1½ teaspoons cayenne pepper

300 ml/10 fl oz coconut milk, from a well-shaken can

Put the oil in a large, heavy pan and set over a medium–high heat. When hot, put in the cinnamon sticks, peppercorns, cloves and cardamom. Let the spices sizzle for a few seconds. Put in the onion. Stir and fry until it turns light brown. Add the curry leaves and ginger. Stir for 1 minute. Add the lamb and stir it around for 3–4 minutes. Now put in 1 litre/32 fl oz water and bring to the boil. Cover, lower the heat and simmer for 30 minutes.

Add the potatoes, carrots, salt and cayenne pepper. Stir and bring to the boil. Cover, lower the heat and cook gently for 40 minutes, or until the meat is tender. Add the coconut milk and crush a few of the potato pieces against the sides of the pan to thicken the sauce. Stir and bring to a simmer.

Rajasthani Red Meat

When this dish is served in the Rajasthan desert region of India, its colour, coming mainly from ground hot chillies, is a fiery red. I have moderated the heat by mixing cayenne pepper with more calming sweet paprika. Use a nice red paprika if you want the proper colour. This is generally served with Indian flatbreads, but rice would be fine too. A calming green vegetable, such as spinach or Swiss chard, could be served on the side. For more robust flavours, have one of the aubergine dishes with it **Serves 4–6**

4 tablespoons olive or rapeseed oil

2 x 7.5-cm/3-inch cinnamon sticks

6 cloves

10 cardamom pods

1 large red onion, peeled and finely chopped

2 teaspoons peeled and very finely grated fresh ginger

4 cloves garlic, peeled and crushed

1 tablespoon ground coriander

900 g/2 lb stewing lamb, preferably from the shoulder

1½ teaspoons salt, or to taste

½–1 teaspoon cayenne pepper

2 tablespoons sweet red paprika

3 tablespoons chopped fresh coriander

Put the oil in a large, heavy pan and set over a medium–high heat. When hot, put in the cinnamon sticks, cloves and cardamom. Let the spices sizzle for a few seconds. Put in the onion. Stir and fry until it turns a reddish-brown. Add the ginger, garlic and coriander. Stir for 1 minute.

Add the lamb, salt, cayenne pepper and paprika. Stir the lamb around for 3–4 minutes. Now put in 1 litre/32 fl oz water and bring to the boil. Cover, lower the heat and simmer for about 1 hour and 10 minutes, or until the meat is tender. Sprinkle the fresh coriander over the top when serving.

Lamb Korma in an Almond-saffron Sauce

The quantities in this recipe may be easily doubled to serve more people. I just love this with Tomato Pullao (see page 206) **Serves 3–4**

4 tablespoons slivered blanched almonds

2.5-cm/1-inch piece of fresh ginger, peeled and chopped

2 good-sized cloves garlic, peeled and chopped

3 tablespoons olive or rapeseed oil

1 x 5–7.5-cm/2–3-inch cinnamon stick

8 cardamom pods

5 cloves

2 bay leaves

560 g/1¼ lb boneless lamb, preferably from the shoulder, cut into 2.5–4-cm/1–1½-inch cubes

¾ teaspoon cayenne pepper

1¼ teaspoons salt

½ teaspoon saffron threads, crumbled

120 ml/4 fl oz single cream

Soak the almonds in 120 ml/4 fl oz boiling water for 2 hours. Put the almonds, their soaking liquid, the ginger and garlic into a blender and blend until smooth.

Put the oil into a medium pan and set over a medium–high heat. When hot, put in the cinnamon, cardamom, cloves and bay leaves. Stir for 5 seconds. Put in half the meat and brown on all sides. Remove the meat with tongs and put in a bowl. Brown the remaining meat in the same way.

Put the first lot of browned meat back into the pan. Pour in the mixture from the blender. Add the cayenne pepper, salt, saffron and 750 ml/24 fl oz cold water. Stir and bring to a simmer. Cover, lower the heat and simmer gently for 60–75 minutes, or until the meat is tender. Add the cream and cook over a medium–high heat for a few minutes so that the sauce is thick.

Lamb Shanks Braised with Cardamom & Onion

Lamb shanks make for some of the best braised meat. The bone and marrow enrich the sauce, and the gelatinous nature of the meat nearest the bone gives it a silken texture. In India we braise shanks in dozens of ways. Muslim families sometimes eat them for breakfast with all manner of flatbreads and raw onion relishes. You could serve them with rice as well, such as Yellow Basmati Rice with Sesame Seeds (see page 202). **Serves 4**

4 medium lamb shanks (about 1.5 kg/3½ lb in total)

salt and freshly ground black pepper

350 ml/12 fl oz natural yoghurt, preferably 'bio' or Greek

6 cloves garlic, peeled and chopped

7.5-cm/3-inch piece of fresh ginger, peeled and chopped

3 tablespoons ground coriander

2 teaspoons ground cumin

½ teaspoon cayenne pepper

4 tablespoons olive or rapeseed oil

10 cardamom pods

½ teaspoon black peppercorns

2 x 7.5-cm/3-inch cinnamon sticks

½ teaspoon whole cloves

1 medium onion, peeled and sliced into fine half-rings

Pat the lamb shanks dry with kitchen paper. Sprinkle them all over with ½ teaspoon salt and lots of freshly ground black pepper.

Preheat the oven to 160°C/gas mark 3.

Put 120 ml/4 fl oz of the yoghurt, the garlic and ginger into a blender and blend until smooth. Now add the coriander, cumin, cayenne pepper, 1½ teaspoons salt and the remaining 230 ml/8 fl oz yoghurt. Blend to mix.

Put the oil in a very wide, flameproof sauté pan or casserole, large enough to hold the shanks easily, and set over a medium–high heat. When hot, put in the cardamon, peppercorns, cinnamon, cloves and the shanks and brown them on one side. Turn them over, dropping the onion slices in the spaces between them. Brown both meat and onions, moving them around the pan as you need to. When the second side of the shanks has browned, add the paste from the blender and 250 ml/8 fl oz water. Bring to the boil.

Cover the pan and place in the oven for 3 hours, turning the shanks over every 30 minutes.

Anglo–Indian Sausage Patties

An Anglo–Indian acquaintance in Calcutta once told me that when he went to buy his sausages from the family butcher, he always took along the spices he wanted as flavouring. He handed these to the butcher and then watched as his choice of meat was minced, seasoned and pushed into casings. I made a note of the recipe and now make those sausages all the time, but I do not always bother with the casings: I make sausage patties instead. We eat these with eggs on Sundays, ensconced between slices of bread as sandwiches, or I put them into a curry (see next recipe), just as Anglo–Indian families have being doing over the years **Makes 8 patties**

450 g/1 lb minced pork, preferably a bit fatty

3 tablespoons peeled and finely chopped shallots or red onions

100 g/3½ oz chopped fresh coriander (see introduction to Green Lamb Curry, page 120)

½–¾ teaspoon cayenne pepper

1 teaspoon garam masala, preferably home-made (see page 264), but shop-bought will do

1 teaspoon salt

freshly ground black pepper

2 teaspoons olive or rapeseed oil

Put the pork in a bowl. Add the shallots, coriander, cayenne pepper, garam masala, salt and lots of black pepper. Mix thoroughly, making sure to pick up and integrate all the shallot and coriander. Shape into a loaf, wrap in cling film and refrigerate, ideally overnight, but for 1–2 hours if you are rushed. Divide into 8 equal pieces and roll into balls. Flatten with the palm of your hand to make 8 smooth patties about 7.5 cm/3 inches in diameter.

Put the oil in a non-stick frying pan and set over a medium–high heat. Put in the patties, as many as will fit easily, and brown on both sides, turning frequently. This will take 4–5 minutes. Make sure that they are cooked through. Make all the patties in this way. Remove with a slotted spatula.

Anglo–Indian Sausage Curry

You need the patties from the preceding recipe and the same pan used for browning them with its leftover oil. This makes for a quick curry, good with rice, bread and also with fried eggs and toast! For a simple meal, serve with a rice dish and vegetable, such as Corn with Aromatic Seasonings (see page 149) or roasted sweet potatoes and a hearty green. **Serves 3–4**

1 quantity Anglo–Indian Sausage Patties (see page 127)

2 tablespoons olive or rapeseed oil

1 medium onion, peeled and finely chopped

1 teaspoon peeled and finely grated fresh ginger

2 cloves garlic, peeled and crushed

4 medium tomatoes, coarsely grated (see page 267) or peeled and finely chopped

½ teaspoon ground turmeric

½ teaspoon salt, or to taste

freshly ground black pepper

4–5 fresh, hot green chillies (such as bird's eye), slit from the bottom to halfway up

Set the cooked patties aside on a plate.

Put the oil into the pattie pan and set over a medium–high heat. When hot, put in the onion. Stir and fry until lightly browned. Add the ginger and garlic. Stir for 1 minute. Put in the tomatoes and turmeric. Stir and cook over a medium–high heat for 3 minutes, or until the sauce has thickened and caramelised a bit. Now add 250 ml/8 fl oz water and the salt, pepper and chillies. Stir and bring to a simmer. Cover, lower the heat and simmer gently for 5 minutes.

Put the sausage patties back into the pan in a single layer if possible, spoon the sauce over to cover them and heat through.

Pork (or Lamb) with Lentils

Indians love dried beans and split peas, eating them in some form at every single meal. They are sometimes cooked on their own, but they can also be combined with vegetables, fish or meat. Ideally, make this dish ahead of time as the lentils absorb a lot of liquid after the cooking is done. Served with a salad and relishes, this dish becomes a meal in itself. **Serves 4**

2 teaspoons ground cumin seeds

4 teaspoons ground coriander seeds

½ teaspoon ground turmeric

½ teaspoon cayenne pepper

3 tablespoons olive or rapeseed oil

50 g/1¾ oz peeled and finely chopped onions

1 teaspoon peeled and finely grated fresh ginger

225 g/8 oz finely chopped tomatoes

675 g/1½ lb boneless shoulder pork, cut into 4-cm/1½-inch cubes

200 g/6¾ oz green lentils, washed and drained

1½ teaspoons salt, or to taste

Combine the cumin, coriander, turmeric and cayenne pepper in a small bowl. Add 2 tablespoons water. Stir to mix.

Put the oil in a large, wide pan and set over a medium heat. When hot, put in the onions. Stir and sauté for about 3 minutes, until the edges are brown. Put in the ginger and stir for 30 seconds. Add the spice paste and stir for 1 minute. Add the tomatoes, stirring for 2–3 minutes. Add the meat, stirring for 2–3 minutes. Pour in 250 ml/8 fl oz water and bring to the boil. Cover and cook over a medium–high heat for 10 minutes, scraping up the sediment now and then. When the sauce is greatly reduced, add the lentils, 900 ml/32 fl oz water and the salt. Stir and bring to a simmer. Cover partially and cook for 40 minutes, or until the lentils are tender. Check for salt, adding more if needed.

Hot, Salty & Sweet Pork Chops

Chinese influence in India is ancient – the two nations have been trading since before the time of Christ. The older Chinese restaurants in the major cities serve an Indianised version of Chinese food, so Indians at home think nothing of adding a bit of soy sauce to this and that. Here is one such modern dish. Ideally, it should be marinated overnight, but a minimum time is suggested below. Plain Jasmine Rice (see page 211) and any vegetable dish would be perfect with these chops. **Serves 4**

For the marinade

¼ teaspoon salt

½ tablespoon whole coriander seeds

2 teaspoons whole cumin seeds

1 x 5-cm/2-inch cinnamon stick

1 teaspoon whole fennel seeds

1 teaspoon whole black peppercorns

½ teaspoon cayenne pepper

To cook the pork

3 tablespoons olive or rapeseed oil

4 centre-cut pork chops (about 900 g/2 lb in total), cut 7.5 mm /⅓ inch thick

½ medium onion, peeled and chopped

1 teaspoon peeled and finely grated fresh ginger

3 tablespoons soy sauce

1½ tablespoons caster sugar

Put all the ingredients for the marinade in a clean coffee- or spice-grinder and grind as finely as possible. Sprinkle the spice mixture evenly over both sides of the pork chops and pat them in. Cover and refrigerate for at least 6 hours, or up to 24 hours.

Put the oil in a large frying pan and set over a medium–high heat. When hot, put in the chops and brown on both sides. Transfer to a bowl.

Put the onion in the pan, lowering the heat a bit, and fry until brown. Add the ginger and stir once. Add the chops in a single layer, then the soy sauce, sugar and 250 ml/8 fl oz water. Bring to the boil. Cover, lower the heat and simmer gently for 50 minutes, or until the chops are tender, turning them every 10 minutes. Reduce the sauce until it is syrupy and clings to the chops.

Pakistani Goat Curry with Potatoes

While this recipe is made with a mixture of boned and unboned goat meat, it can also be made with lamb shoulder, some of which is unboned. Good lamb generally takes about 50–80 minutes to cook, less time than goat. At home in India we ate this everyday dish with Chapatis (see page 222). And there was always a dal, such as My Everyday Moong Dal (see page 192), a couple of vegetables and some relishes and chutneys. You can, of course, serve a simple rice dish instead of the bread. **Serves 4**

4 tablespoons olive oil, rapeseed oil or ghee

2 x 5-cm/2-inch cinnamon sticks

8 whole cardamom pods

1 large red onion, peeled and sliced into very fine half-rings

3 cloves garlic, peeled and crushed

1 tablespoon peeled and very finely chopped fresh ginger

1.35 kg/3 lb goat meat (see page 108)

¼ teaspoon ground turmeric

1 tablespoon ground coriander

¼–½ teaspoon cayenne pepper

6 egg-sized potatoes (about 450 g/1 lb in total), peeled and left whole

2 teaspoons salt

1 teaspoon garam masala, preferably home-made (see page 264), but shop-bought will do

Put the oil in a wide, heavy pan and set over a medium–high heat. When hot, put in the cinnamon, cardamom and onion. Stir and fry for 5–6 minutes, or until the onions turn a light brown. Add the garlic and ginger. Stir for 1 minute. Add the meat, turmeric, coriander and cayenne pepper. Stir for 2–3 minutes. Add 250 ml/8 fl oz water and bring to the boil. Cover and cook over a medium heat for about 10 minutes, or until all the liquid has evaporated. Remove the cover and stir for 3–4 minutes to brown the meat slightly. Now add 1 litre /32 fl oz water and bring to the boil. Cover, lower the heat and cook gently for 1 hour.

Add the potatoes and salt. Stir and bring to the boil. Cover, lower the heat and cook gently for another 30 minutes, or until the meat is very tender. Sprinkle the garam masala over the top and mix in. Turn off the heat.

Beef or Lamb Jhal Faraizi

This dish is a speciality of the Anglo–Indian community and probably started as a way to use up leftover roast lamb or beef. When there were no leftovers and there was a craving for the dish, fresh meat was diced small and boiled with a little salt and ginger until it was tender and this was used instead. These days if you don't have leftovers, you can buy roast beef from a delicatessen (ask them to cut the slices 7 mm/⅓ inch thick – you will need just a few). *Jhal* means 'heat from hot chillies', so chillies are an essential ingredient. I found this recipe in an old Anglo–Indian cookery book in Calcutta, and it's the one I like best. It's something like a hash brown, only spicy. This can be served for breakfast with or without eggs, or by itself with a salad **Serves 2–4**

340 g/12 oz flourty potatoes, unpeeled

2 tablespoons olive or rapeseed oil

½ teaspoon whole cumin seeds

1 medium onion, peeled and cut into 7-mm/⅓-inch dice

2–3 fresh, hot green chillies (such as bird's eye), chopped

340 g/12 oz roast beef or lamb, cut into 7-mm/⅓-inch dice

1 teaspoon salt

freshly ground black pepper

Boil the potatoes ahead of time and set aside to cool. Peel them and then cut into 7-mm/⅓-inch dice.

Put the oil in a large frying pan, preferably non-stick, and set over a medium–high heat. When hot, put in the cumin seeds. Let them sizzle for 5 seconds. Add the onion, potatoes and chillies. Lower the heat to medium. Stir and fry for about 5 minutes, or until the onion turns somewhat translucent. Now add the meat, salt and lots of black pepper. Stir and mix for 1 minute. Reduce the heat to medium–low. Press down on all the ingredients with a spatula to form a flat cake that fills the pan. Cook for about 15 minutes, shifting and turning the pan so that the bottom of the 'cake' browns evenly. Break it up and serve hot.

Baked Beef Curry

Beef is eaten by Muslims throughout India, Pakistan and Bangladesh, and is often referred to as *bara gosht* (big meat). It is sometimes 'baked' using an ancient hob method known as *dum* (see page 116). However, a conventional oven can produce similar results. Serve with rice or Indian breads. Black Beans (see page 182) could be served on the side, along with vegetables and relishes for an elegant meal   **Serves 4–6**

6 tablespoons olive or rapeseed oil

6 cardamom pods

2 x 5-cm/2-inch cinnamon sticks

900 g/2 lb stewing beef, cut into 4-cm/1½-inch pieces

1 teaspoon whole cumin seeds

225 g/8 oz peeled and chopped onions

300 ml/10 fl oz natural yoghurt, lightly beaten

2 tablespoons ground coriander

2 teaspoons peeled and finely grated fresh ginger or 1 teaspoon ground ginger

¼–½ teaspoon cayenne pepper

1½ teaspoons salt, or to taste

Preheat the oven to 180°C/gas mark 4.

Put the oil into a wide, flameproof casserole and set over a medium–high heat. When hot, put in the cardamom and cinnamon. Stir once, then add only as much of the meat as will brown easily. Brown on all sides. Using a slotted spoon, transfer to a bowl. Brown the remaining meat in the same way and add to the bowl.

Add the cumin seeds and onions to the casserole and fry until the onions just begin to brown. Turn off the heat.

Return the meat and its accumulated juices to the casserole. Add all the remaining ingredients. Stir to mix and bring to a simmer. Cover first with foil, crimping the edges, and then with a lid. Place in the oven for 1½ hours, or until the meat is tender.

Calves' Liver with Onion

Here I have taken a Pakistani recipe for stir-fried liver made in the wok-like *karhai* and changed it just enough so that Westerners, who like their liver softer and pinker than South Asians, may enjoy it too. If you want the Pakistani recipe, after the liver has browned, cut it crossways into 2.5-cm/1-inch squares and add these pieces to the onion sauce when it is ready. Continue to stir and cook over a low heat until the liver is done to your liking. Serve with rice and a salad or a green vegetable **Serves 2**

2 slices of calves' liver (about 340 g/12 oz in total)

salt

¼ teaspoon ground turmeric

⅛ teaspoon cayenne pepper

3 tablespoons olive or rapeseed oil

¼ teaspoon whole cumin seeds

1 large onion, peeled and sliced into 5-mm/¼-inch half-rings

1 clove garlic, peeled and crushed

½ teaspoon mustard powder

1 medium tomato, grated

1 fresh, hot green chilli (such as bird's eye), finely chopped (optional)

freshly ground black pepper

1–2 teaspoons lemon juice

Lay the liver slices down flat and rub ¼ teaspoon salt, the turmeric and cayenne pepper on both sides. Cover and set aside for 30 minutes. (All the other ingredients may be prepared during this time.)

Put 1 tablespoon of the oil in a non-stick frying pan and set over a medium–high heat. When hot, put in the liver slices. Cook the first side until browned, about 1½–2 minutes. Turn the slices over and cook the second side in the same way. If you want the slices a bit more done, lower the heat to medium and cook both sides for 30–60 seconds longer. Transfer to a serving dish and keep warm.

Add the remaining 2 tablespoons oil to the frying pan and set over a medium–high heat. When hot, put in the cumin seeds. Ten seconds later, put in the onion. Stir a few times and lower the heat to medium. Stir and fry the onion for 6–8 minutes, or until softened a bit and browned slightly on the edges. Add the garlic and stir a few times. Now put in the mustard powder, tomato, chilli, black pepper, lemon juice and ¼–⅓ teaspoon salt. Stir and cook for 1 minute. Pour this sauce on top of the liver slices and serve.

Sri Lankan Beef Smore

Here we have a speciality of Sri Lanka's Burgher community, which owes its origins to a happy mixture of European colonialists, mostly Dutch but some Portuguese and English as well, with the local population. Burgher cuisine is a glorious by-product of this union. This simple pot-roast has been made wonderfully Sri Lankan with the addition of roasted coriander, cumin and fennel seeds, the main ingredients in Sri Lankan curry powders, and, of course, coconut milk. Some people also add a little lime pickle or tamarind water or vinegar to give it a tart edge. I have used red wine vinegar. When ready, the meat is sliced and served with some of its own sauce ladled over the top. Serve with rice or noodles or mashed potatoes **Serves 4–6**

1 x 1.25-kg/2½-lb piece of beef suitable for braising, e.g. shoulder meat tied as a roast, or a piece of chuck, or even brisket

salt and freshly ground black pepper

4 teaspoons whole coriander seeds

1 teaspoon whole cumin seeds

1 teaspoon whole fennel seeds

¼ teaspoon whole fenugreek seeds

4 tablespoons olive or rapeseed oil

1 x 5-cm/2-inch cinnamon stick

1 large onion, peeled and finely chopped

5-cm/2-inch piece of fresh ginger, peeled and finely grated

4 cloves garlic, peeled and finely chopped

2 tablespoons red wine vinegar

350 ml/12 fl oz beef or chicken stock

½–1 teaspoon cayenne pepper

250 ml/8 fl oz coconut milk, from a well-shaken can

Pat the meat dry with kitchen paper, then sprinkle lightly with salt and lots of black pepper.

Put a small heavy-based frying pan over a medium heat. When very hot, put in the coriander, cumin, fennel and fenugreek seeds. Stir for 30 seconds or so until the spices just start to emit a roasted aroma. Empty on to a piece of kitchen paper and allow to cool a bit. Grind in a clean coffee- or spice-grinder, or crush in a mortar.

Preheat the oven to 160°C/gas mark 3.

Put the oil in a flameproof casserole and set over a medium–high heat. When hot, put in the meat and brown on all sides. Transfer to a plate. Return the casserole to the heat and add the cinnamon, onion, ginger and garlic. Stir and cook for 4–5 minutes. Add the vinegar, stock, cayenne pepper, 1½ teaspoons salt, the roasted, ground spices and the beef with its accumulated juices. Bring to the boil, stirring the sauce. Cover and place in oven. Cook, basting and turning every 20 minutes or so, for 2–2½ hours, or until the meat is tender.

Transfer the casserole to the hob. Add the coconut milk, stir and bring to a simmer before serving.

Vegetables

India has some of the best-tasting vegetables in the world, all available fresh daily at very reasonable prices. Indian tomatoes – and here I include those found in Pakistan, Sri Lanka and Bangladesh – may look squiggly and misshapen, but they have better texture and flavour than what I find much of the year in Britain and the United States. The same holds true for cabbage, cauliflower and almost any other vegetable you can name. Southern Asia eats many more types of vegetable too. From snake gourds to wing beans, green plantains to green jackfruit, the best vegetables from around the world have found their way here and each is cooked in hundreds of different ways.

Green beans may be cooked very simply with mustard, cumin and sesame seeds; winter carrots are often just sliced and stir-fried with fresh fenugreek greens or, failing that, with coriander; monsoon corn is either roasted, like chestnuts, or its grains stir-fried with green chillies, ginger, cinnamon and cardamom. Then there are aubergines, a very popular 'meaty' vegetable that is thought to have originated in India. It is fried into fritters, partially quartered and stuffed, combined with dumplings, made into pilafs, stewed with tomatoes, cooked with quinces, roasted and put into yoghurt raitas – I could do a whole book of South Asian aubergine recipes! I could do the same with potato.

Even though potatoes came to India from the West, the nation took to them like ducks to water. One wit in Calcutta remarked that the only good thing the British ever gave to India was the potato. Its starchy texture lent itself beautifully to south Asia's array of spices: it was stewed with tomatoes and ginger, stir-fried with asafoetida and cumin, combined with peas and cauliflower, and made into curries flavoured with chillies and mustard seeds.

For this chapter, I have selected more than two dozen of the simpler recipes, all for vegetables that can be found easily in the West. They will provide endless variety for vegetarian diets. Meat- and fish-eaters will be able to spice up entire meals with new aromas, textures and tastes. And here is another thing: you should not feel obliged to make a complete Indian meal every time you want to cook one of these vegetable dishes. Next time you have grilled chicken, for example, try an Indian potato dish instead of boiled potatoes; have an Indian corn dish with frankfurters or sausages. Feel free to mix and match – anything to make your life easier and your meals more exciting.

Aubergines with Tomatoes

Although aubergines come in various colours, I use the purple kind for this recipe. Normally, aubergine chunks require frying first to give their unctuous, satiny texture, after which they may be folded into a variety of sauces. But I have found a less oily way of preparing them: I grill them instead. Serve hot with a lamb or chicken curry, or as a cold salad with cold meats, such as Tandoori-style Chicken with Mint (see page 85) **Serves 4–6**

5 medium-sized aubergines (about 140 g/5 oz each), cut into 5 x 2.5-cm/2 x 1-inch chunks with skin on at least one side

salt

5 tablespoons olive, rapeseed or peanut oil

1 teaspoon whole black or yellow mustard seeds

½ teaspoon whole cumin seeds

½ teaspoon whole fennel seeds

½ teaspoon whole nigella seeds (kalonji), if available

1 hot, dried red chilli

2 cloves garlic, peeled and chopped

340 g/12 oz peeled and chopped tomatoes (see page 267)

¼ teaspoon caster sugar

Preheat the grill to its highest setting, positioning a shelf so it is 13–15 cm/5–6 inches from the source of the heat.

Spread out the aubergine chunks in a baking tin. Sprinkle them with ½ teaspoon salt and 2 tablespoons of the oil. Toss and put under the grill for about 15 minutes, tossing now and then, until all sides are lightly browned.

Put the remaining 3 tablespoons oil in a large sauté pan and set over a medium–high heat. When hot, put in all the seeds and the chilli. As soon as the mustard seeds begin to pop, a matter of seconds, put in the garlic. Stir a few times until golden, then quickly add the tomatoes, the grilled aubergine, ¼ teaspoon salt and the sugar. Mix and bring to a simmer. Cover, lower the heat and simmer gently for about 20 minutes, stirring now and then, until the aubergines are tender and smothered in the sauce.

Sweet & Sour Aubergines

Aubergines come in so many sizes and shapes. Here you can use four 'baby' Italian aubergines, four Japanese, or eight of the very small Indian ones. All are partially quartered – the top, stem and sepal end always stay attached so that the aubergines retain their shape – and then stuffed with a spice mixture before being cooked. For the spice mixture to hold, a little starch needs to be added. In India this is the very nutritious chickpea flour. Cornmeal or *masa harina* can be used instead if you have them to hand. This very gratifying dish may be served as a main course, along with a green vegetable, some dal (such as Black Beans, see page 182), rice and a yoghurt relish. It would also go well with hearty chicken and lamb curries **Serves 4**

4 purple baby aubergines (aim for 560g/1¼ lb) or see above

2 tablespoons chickpea flour

1 teaspoon peeled and very finely grated fresh ginger

¼–½ teaspoon cayenne pepper

1½ tablespoons ground coriander

1 teaspoon ground cumin

salt

3 tablespoons finely chopped fresh coriander

4 tablespoons olive or rapeseed oil

2 teaspoons caster sugar

2 teaspoons lemon juice

Cut the aubergines lengthways into quarters, holding them together by not cutting through the stem end. Leave to soak in a bowl of water for 30 minutes.

Put the flour in a small, cast-iron frying pan. Stir over a medium heat until it is a shade darker. Transfer to a small bowl. Add the ginger, cayenne pepper, ground coriander, cumin, ¾ teaspoon salt, fresh coriander and 4 tablespoons water. Stir to make a paste.

Drain the aubergines and dry them with kitchen paper. Rub the spice mixture on all the cut surfaces.

Put the oil in a medium frying pan and set over a medium–high heat. When hot, put in the aubergines and brown them lightly on all sides. Sprinkle ¼ teaspoon salt over the top and add 4 tablespoons water. Bring to a simmer. Cover, lower the heat and cook gently for 25 minutes or until tender.

Meanwhile, combine 4 tablespoons water with the sugar and lemon juice. Pour this over the aubergines when they are tender. Continue cooking over a medium–high heat, turning them gently once, until you have a thick sauce at the bottom, about 2–3 minutes.

Aubergines in a North–south Sauce

This is one of our most beloved family dishes. It is very much in the Hyderabadi style, where Indian seasonings from north and south are combined. Over the years, I have simplified the recipe. Here you may use long, tender Japanese aubergines or Italian purple 'baby' aubergines, or even the striated purple and white ones that are about the same size as the baby ones. The aim is to cut chunks with as much skin on them as possible so that they do not fall apart. Serve hot with meat or vegetable curries plus rice and dal, or serve cold, as a salad, with cold meats. It's good with Chicken Karhai with Mint (see page 176), and I love it with slices of ham **Serves 4–6**

4 tablespoons olive or rapeseed oil

⅛ teaspoon ground asafoetida

½ teaspoon skinned urad dal or yellow split peas

½ teaspoon whole mustard seeds

½ teaspoon whole cumin seeds

½ teaspoon whole nigella seeds (kalonji), if available

½ teaspoon whole fennel seeds

1 medium onion, peeled and chopped

2 cloves garlic, peeled and chopped

675 g/1½ lb aubergines (see above), cut into 2.5-cm/1-inch chunks (baby aubergines should be cut in half lengthways first)

2 medium tomatoes, grated (about 300 ml/10 fl oz – see page 267)

250 ml/8 fl oz chicken stock or water

1 teaspoon salt

¼–½ teaspoon cayenne pepper

Pour the oil into a very large frying pan and set over a medium–high heat. When hot, put in the asafoetida and the urad dal. As soon as the dal turns a shade darker, add the mustard, cumin, nigella and fennel seeds in that order. When the mustard seeds begin to pop, a matter of seconds, add the onion. Stir and fry for 1 minute. Add the garlic and the aubergines. Stir and fry for 4–5 minutes, or until the onions are lightly browned.

Add the tomatoes, stock, salt and cayenne pepper. Stir to mix and bring to the boil. Cover, lower the heat and cook gently for about 20 minutes, or until the aubergines are tender, stirring now and then.

Aubergines in a North–south Sesame or Peanut Sauce

2 tablespoons sesame paste (tahini) or peanut butter

120 ml/4 fl oz chicken stock or water

Follow the instructions above, but 10 minutes before the cooking time is up, put the sesame paste (tahini) or peanut butter in a small bowl. Slowly add the chicken stock or water and mix well. Add this mixture to the pan and stir in. Cover and continue cooking gently until the aubergines are tender.

South Indian-style Green Beans

Vegetables are often very simply prepared in southern India. Here they are blanched and then quickly stir-fried with spices. These beans can be served with any meat, poultry or fish dish, whether South Asian or Western **Serves 4**

450 g/1 lb green beans, trimmed and cut into 2.5-cm/1-inch lengths

salt

3 tablespoons olive or rapeseed oil

½ teaspoon whole cumin seeds

½ teaspoon whole brown or yellow mustard seeds

½ teaspoon whole sesame seeds

⅛ teaspoon cayenne pepper

Bring 2 litres/70 fl oz water to the boil. Add 1 tablespoon salt and then the beans. Boil for 4–5 minutes, or until the beans are just tender. Drain immediately and leave in the colander.

Put the oil in a frying pan and set over a medium–high heat. When hot, put in the cumin, mustard and sesame seeds. As soon as the seeds start popping, a matter of seconds, take the pan off the heat and add the beans. Stir. Put the pan back on the hob, turning the heat down to medium–low. Stir for about 1 minute, adding ½ teaspoon salt and the cayenne pepper. Serve immediately.

Karhai Broccoli

Broccoli, once unknown in India, is now found in many specialist markets. I use a nice-sized bunch and keep the better part of the stems as well, after peeling them and cutting them crossways into thickish slices. Cut the broccoli head into small florets, each no longer than 4 cm/1½ inches, leaving a bit of stem attached so that they retain their elegance. Serve this versatile dish at either Indian or Western meals **Serves 4**

3 tablespoons olive or
   rapeseed oil

⅛ teaspoon ground asafoetida

¼ teaspoon whole cumin seeds

¼ teaspoon whole mustard
   seeds

400 g/14 oz trimmed and cut
   broccoli (see above)

½ teaspoon salt

¼ teaspoon cayenne pepper

Put the oil into a *karhai*, wok or medium frying pan and set over a medium–high heat. When hot, put in the asafoetida and then the cumin and mustard seeds. As soon as the mustard seeds begin to pop, a matter of seconds, put in the broccoli. Stir and fry for 1 minute, adding the salt and cayenne pepper as you do so. Pour in 4 tablespoons water and bring to a simmer. Cover, lower the heat and cook for 7–8 minutes, or until the broccoli is just tender, stirring now and then.

Swiss Chard with Ginger & Garlic

Indians love eating greens at all meals. In northern India the greens are often cooked simply, with ginger, garlic and chilli powder or green chillies. These greens go well with meats. If you are having a simple Indian meal of dal and rice, all you need to add is a green vegetable and a relish, perhaps with yoghurt in it **Serves 4**

675 g/1½ lb Swiss chard, well washed

3 tablespoons olive or rapeseed oil

1 clove garlic, peeled and cut into long slivers

1 teaspoon peeled and finely slivered fresh ginger (see page 265)

½ teaspoon salt

¼ teaspoon cayenne pepper

Holding several leaves together and starting at the stem end, cut the chard crossways at 5-mm/¼-inch intervals.

Pour the oil into a large pan and place over a medium–high heat. When hot, put in the garlic and ginger. Stir a few times. Put in all the chard, with the washing water still clinging to the leaves. Cover. As soon as the leaves have wilted, a matter of a few minutes, add the salt and cayenne pepper. Stir to mix. Cover again and lower the heat. Cook for 5 minutes, or until the chard is just done.

Corn with Aromatic Seasonings

Here is a fragrant and easy stir-fried corn dish that can be made with fresh or frozen corn. This may be served with most Indian meals, but also goes well with Western-style roast or grilled pork, duck and chicken **Serves 4–6**

3 tablespoons olive or rapeseed oil

1 teaspoon whole brown or yellow mustard seeds

4 cardamom pods

4 cloves

2.5-cm/1-inch piece of cinnamon stick

2 bay leaves

1 teaspoon peeled and finely grated fresh ginger

1–2 teaspoons finely chopped fresh, hot green chilli (do not discard seeds)

560 g/1¼ lb corn kernels, defrosted and drained if frozen

1 teaspoon salt

150 ml/5 fl oz single cream

Pour the oil into a frying pan and set over a medium heat. Meanwhile, combine the mustard seeds, cardamom, cloves, cinnamon and bay leaves in a small bowl. When the oil is hot, add the bowl of spices. As soon as the mustard seeds pop, a matter of seconds, put in the ginger and chilli. Stir once or twice, then add the corn. Stir for 2–3 minutes. Add the salt and cream. Continue to stir and cook for another minute. Lower the heat and cook for 1–2 minutes, stirring, until all the cream is absorbed.

Before serving, pick out and discard the cardamom pods, cloves, cinnamon and bay leaves.

Carrots with Coriander

This recipe is an everyday carrot dish. In India it is served hot, but I often serve it cold in the summer, almost like a carrot salad **Serves 4**

2 tablespoons peanut or olive oil

⅛ teaspoon ground asafoetida

¼ teaspoon whole cumin seeds

450 g/1 lb carrots, peeled and cut into rounds 7 mm/⅓ inch thick

60 g/2 oz very finely chopped fresh coriander

½ teaspoon salt

⅛–¼ teaspoon cayenne pepper

Put the oil in a medium frying pan and set over a medium–high heat. When hot, put in the asafoetida and cumin seeds. Stir once or twice, then add the carrots. Stir once and turn off the heat. Add all the remaining ingredients and 3 tablespoons water. Stir well and bring to a simmer over a medium heat. Cover, reduce the heat to very low and simmer very gently for 3–4 minutes, or until the carrots are done, stirring once or twice during this time.

Courgettes & Yellow Summer Squash with Cumin

Here is how my family in India prepared our everyday summer marrows and squashes. It was utterly simple and utterly good. The squash used was shaped liked a bowling pin and slightly curled up, but the taste and texture were similar to other types. I like to use both yellow squash and courgettes together, but you could use just one or the other. This may be served hot at most Indian meals, or cold as a salad **Serves 4–6**

2 medium courgettes and 2 medium yellow squash (about 675 g/1½ lb in total)

4 tablespoons olive or rapeseed oil

generous pinch of ground asafoetida

1 teaspoon whole cumin seeds

180 g/6 oz finely chopped tomatoes

1 teaspoon salt

⅛ teaspoon cayenne pepper

Trim the courgettes and squash, then quarter them lengthways. Cut them crossways into 2.5-cm/1-inch chunks.

Pour the oil into a frying pan and set over a medium heat. When hot, put in the asafoetida and cumin seeds. Stir once, then put in the tomatoes. Stir and cook for about 2 minutes, or until the tomatoes have softened. Add all the courgettes and squash. Stir and sauté for 2 minutes. Add the salt, cayenne pepper and 4 tablespoons water. Stir to mix, and bring to a simmer. Cover, reduce the heat to medium–low and cook, stirring once or twice, for 5–6 minutes, or until the vegetables are just done.

Sri Lankan White Courgette Curry

Even though this is called a white curry, it is slightly yellowish from the small amount of turmeric in it. In Sri Lanka it is made with ridge gourd, which looks like a ridged, slightly curved cucumber, pointy at the ends. This is sold in Indian, South-east Asian and Chinese shops. If you can find it, peel it with a vegetable peeler, concentrating mostly on the high ridges, and then cut it crossways into 2-cm/¾-inch pieces. It cooks in about 3 minutes. Here I have used courgette instead because it is just as good and easier to find. Serve with rice and perhaps Stir-fried Chettinad Chicken (see page 82) **Serves 4–6**

4 medium courgettes (about 675 g/1½ lb in total)

¼ teaspoon ground turmeric

⅛ teaspoon cayenne pepper

15 fresh curry leaves or 10 fresh basil leaves, torn

½ teaspoon salt

1 medium shallot, peeled and cut into fine slivers

300 ml/10 fl oz coconut milk, from a well-shaken can

Trim the courgettes and cut them in half lengthways, then crossways into 2-cm/¾-inch pieces.

Put the courgettes in a very large frying pan or sauté pan with all the other ingredients and set over a medium–high heat. Stir and bring to a simmer. Lower the heat to medium and cook for about 5 minutes, stirring and spooning the sauce over the courgettes.

Pan-grilled Courgettes

I have not measured out the spices in this recipe as all you do is sprinkle them over the top. A little more or a little less makes hardly any difference. Serve these courgettes with curries or grilled or roasted meats   **Serves 2–4**

4 smallish courgettes (about 450 g/1 lb in total)

4 tablespoons olive or rapeseed oil

lemon juice

salt and freshly ground black pepper

roasted and ground cumin seeds (see page 263)

cayenne pepper

Cut the courgettes in half lengthways.

Pour the oil into a large frying pan and set over a medium–high heat. When hot, put in the courgettes, skin side down, in a single layer. (Do in batches if necessary.) When the skin is a reddish-brown, turn the pieces over. Brown the cut side in the same way. Arrange in a single layer on a platter, cut side up. Squeeze some lemon juice over the top, then sprinkle with salt, lots of black pepper, some cumin and cayenne pepper. Serve immediately.

Kashmiri-style Spring Greens

One of my cousins was married to a Kashmiri gentleman, who for the period when he was working at the United Nations in New York took along a manservant. My cousin let me have him once a week to cook and clean. He made this Kashmiri staple week after week, and it remains one of our favourites. Spring-type greens (of the Brassica family) are commonly eaten in Kashmir, the season for them lasting from spring (when they are tender) until the snows start to fall in early winter (when they are coarser). Note that young greens will cook faster than old ones, so start with half the stock suggested and add more if needed. Serve with rice and either a dal or a meat curry **Serves 6**

800 g/1¾ lb spring greens

3 tablespoons olive or rapeseed oil

⅛ teaspoon ground asafoetida

3 whole hot dried red chillies

450 ml/15 fl oz chicken stock or water

salt

Wash the greens, then remove their stems and coarse central veins. Stack 6–7 leaves on top of each other and roll them up lengthways. Cut crossways to get 1-cm/½-inch ribbons. Now cut lengthways again to get 1-cm/½-inch pieces.

Pour the oil into a large pan and set over a medium–high heat. When hot, put in the asafoetida and the chillies. As soon as the chillies darken, a matter of seconds, take the pan off the heat briefly to add the greens and stock. Put the pan back on the heat and bring to the boil. Cover, reduce the heat to medium–low, and cook for 10–40 minutes, until the greens are tender. Remove the cover and taste. Seasoned stock may require only ½ teaspoon salt to be added. Add what is needed. Increase the heat to medium–high and boil away most of the liquid. If you are eating the greens with rice, you may want to save some extra juice to moisten it adequately.

Mushroom Bhaaji

The term *bhaaji* is often misinterpreted in the UK as many restaurants use it to describe a fritter. In fact the word for a fritter is *bhajia* (see Prawn and Onion fritters, page 27) and the word *bhaji* simply means 'a vegetable dish'. I have chosen to spell it *bhaaji*, with a long 'ah' sound, in this recipe to indicate the correct pronunciation, though it can be spelt with only one 'a'. For this stir-fry I use largish white mushrooms, but if your mushrooms are medium-sized, you should cut them in half rather than quarters.

Serve this *bhaaji* as part of an Indian meal, along with rice or breads, a fish dish and a relish, or have it with scrambled eggs for brunch   **Serves 3–4**

3 tablespoons olive or rapeseed oil

½ teaspoon whole brown mustard seeds

½ teaspoon whole cumin seeds

4 tablespoons peeled and finely chopped onions

285 g/10 oz largish white mushrooms, quartered

1 clove garlic, peeled and crushed

3 tablespoons natural yoghurt

⅛ teaspoon cayenne pepper

1 teaspoon ground coriander

½ teaspoon salt

2 tablespoons finely chopped fresh coriander

Pour the oil into a frying pan and set over a medium heat. When hot, put in the mustard and cumin seeds. As soon as the mustard seeds start to pop, a matter of seconds, put in the onion. Stir and fry until it starts to brown at the edges. Put in the mushrooms and stir for 1 minute. Take the pan off the heat and put in the garlic, yoghurt, cayenne pepper, ground coriander and salt.

Put the pan back over a medium heat and stir well. Keep cooking and stirring until all the yoghurt is absorbed, a few minutes. Stir in the fresh coriander towards the end.

Mushroom & Pea Curry

This is a great curry for vegetarians and meat-eaters alike. I like to use cremini mushrooms, as they have a firmer texture than ordinary ones, but don't worry if you cannot get them – medium-sized white mushrooms will do. Serve with rice or Indian bread and some relishes

Serves 4

1 tablespoon ground coriander

1½ teaspoons ground cumin

¼ teaspoon ground turmeric

¼ teaspoon cayenne pepper

3 tablespoons olive or rapeseed oil

50 g/1¾ oz peeled and finely chopped onion

1 teaspoon peeled and finely grated fresh ginger

225 g/8 oz peeled and finely chopped tomato (a relatively firm tomato can be peeled with a paring knife, like an apple)

1¼ teaspoons salt, or to taste

450 g/1 lb cremini mushrooms, halved lengthways

285 g/10 oz peas, defrosted if frozen

Combine the coriander, cumin, turmeric and cayenne pepper in a small bowl. Add about 1½ tablespoons water and mix to make a paste.

Pour the oil into a medium pan and set over a medium heat. When hot, put in the onion. Stir and sauté for 3–4 minutes, or until the edges begin to brown. Add the ginger and stir 3–4 times. Add the spice paste. Stir and cook for about 1 minute. Add the tomato. Stir and cook, scraping up any sediment from the bottom of the pan, for about 4 minutes, or until the tomato has softened. Add 450 ml/15 fl oz water and the salt. Stir and bring to the boil. Cover, lower the heat and simmer for 20 minutes.

Add the mushrooms to the pan and bring to the boil. Cover and cook over a low heat for 10 minutes. Add the peas and bring back to the boil. Cover and cook over a low heat for 5 minutes, or until the peas are done. Check for salt, adding a bit more if needed.

Gujarati-style Okra

An everyday vegetable dish, this is made in the Gujarati style of western India, without onions. In India this is generally eaten with legume dishes, other vegetables, yoghurt relishes, pickles and breads

Serves 4

3 tablespoons olive or rapeseed oil

generous pinch of ground asafoetida

½ teaspoon whole brown or yellow mustard seeds

450 g/1 lb small, tender okra, cleaned and trimmed as described in following recipe, then cut crossways at 1-cm/½-inch intervals

⅛ teaspoon ground turmeric

1 teaspoon salt

½ teaspoon ground cumin

½ teaspoon ground coriander

¼–½ teaspoon cayenne pepper, or to taste

Pour the oil into a frying pan and set over a medium–high heat. When hot, put in the asafoetida and mustard seeds. As soon as the seeds begin to pop, a matter of seconds, put in the okra. Lower the heat to medium. Stir and cook for 3 minutes. Add the turmeric and salt and toss well. Reduce the heat to medium–low. Stir and cook for 8–9 minutes, or until the okra is lightly browned and almost cooked.

Sprinkle in the cumin, coriander and cayenne pepper. Toss, lower the heat and cook for another 2 minutes.

Okra with Shallots (*Bhuni Bhindi*)

This is easily my favourite okra recipe, though I must admit to loving plain, crisply fried okra as well. As okra has a mucilaginous or slimy quality, it is never washed. Instead, it is wiped with a damp cloth and left to air-dry before being cut. The sliminess is somewhat reduced by careful cooking. In northern Indian pinkish-red onions are the norm, while in the south shallots are used. As shallots seem to be getting larger and larger, I suggest you use about three of the larger ones here. When I was a child, all I wanted for lunch was this okra dish, some Chapatis and My Everyday Moong Dal (see pages 222 and 192) and a yoghurt relish. You may, of course, serve this with meat curries as well   **Serves 4**

340 g/12 oz small, tender okra, cleaned as described above

4 tablespoons olive, rapeseed or peanut oil

½ teaspoon whole cumin seeds

60 g/2 oz shallots or onions, peeled and halved lengthways, then cut into fine half-rings

1½ teaspoons ground coriander

¼ teaspoon crushed dried red chillies

½ teaspoon salt

1 teaspoon lemon juice

Cut off the top stem and very tip of the okra pods (you can do 3–4 at the same time). Now cut each pod diagonally into 3–4 slices, depending upon size.

Pour the oil into a medium frying pan and set over a medium–high heat. When hot, put in the cumin seeds. A few seconds later put in all the sliced okra. Stir and fry for about 5 minutes. The okra will have browned a bit.

Add the shallots to the pan and continue to stir and fry for about 3 minutes until they brown as well. Now lower the heat. Add the coriander, chillies and salt. Stir and cook for another 7–9 minutes, or until the okra is crisp and cooked through. Add the lemon juice and stir to mix.

Potato Chaat

Chaat is a term applied to certain kinds of hot and sour foods that are generally eaten as snacks, but may be served at lunch as well. When I was growing up in Delhi, the servants cooked the main dishes, but it was my mother who always made the chaat. This she would do not in the kitchen, but in the pantry where she kept the seasonings for it, the most important of which was roasted and ground cumin seeds. Chaat could be made out of many things – various boiled tubers, boiled legumes, such as chickpeas and mung beans, and even fruit, such as bananas, green mangoes, guavas and oranges. It is important not to refrigerate this recipe at any stage because refrigeration changes the texture of the potatoes **Serves 4**

675 g/1½ lb waxy potatoes, boiled until just done, cooled thoroughly (without refrigeration) and peeled

1¼ teaspoons salt

¼ teaspoon cayenne pepper, or to taste

freshly ground black pepper

½ teaspoon roasted and ground cumin seeds

1½ tablespoons lemon juice

chopped fresh coriander

Cut the potatoes into 1-cm/½-inch dice and put into a non-reactive (ceramic, glass or stainless steel) bowl. Add all the remaining ingredients and mix well. Taste for balance of spices, adding more of them if you like. Serve at room temperature, with chopped fresh coriander sprinkled over the top.

Potato & Pea Chaat

Once the potatoes have been diced into the bowl, add 140 g/5 oz boiled and well-drained peas. Add just a little bit more of each of the seasonings, tasting to make sure you have a good balance. Serve at room temperature, with chopped fresh coriander sprinkled over the top **Serves 4**

Stir-fried Potato Chaat

Pour 3 tablespoons olive or rapeseed oil into a large non-stick pan and set over a medium–high heat. When hot, put in the cooked Potato Chaat. Stir and fry for 4–5 minutes, until the potatoes are lightly browned. Serve hot, with chopped fresh coriander sprinkled over the top

Serves 4

South Indian Potato Curry

A southern potato curry from the Chennai region, this would be served there with rice. In the north, though, it would be accompanied by a flatbread. Dal and vegetables should be added to the meal   **Serves 4**

3 tablespoons olive or rapeseed oil

1 teaspoon whole brown mustard seeds

½ teaspoon skinned urad dal or yellow split peas

2 whole dried, hot red chillies

15–20 fresh curry leaves or 10 fresh basil leaves, torn

½ medium onion, peeled and chopped

1 medium tomato, chopped

2 teaspoons ground coriander

⅛–¼ teaspoon cayenne pepper

1 teaspoon garam masala, home-made (see page 264) or shop-bought

450 g/1 lb waxy potatoes, peeled and cut into 2-cm/¾-inch dice

1 teaspoon salt

120 ml/4 fl oz coconut milk, from a well-shaken can

4 tablespoons chopped fresh coriander

Pour the oil into a medium pan and set over a medium–high heat. When hot, put in the mustard seeds, urad dal and chillies. As soon as the seeds begin to pop, a matter of seconds, put in the curry leaves and onion. Lower the heat to medium. Stir and fry the onion for about 3 minutes, or until it has softened but not browned.

Add the tomato, ground coriander, cayenne pepper and garam masala. Stir for 1 minute. Add the potatoes and stir another minute. Now put in 250 ml/8 fl oz water and the salt. Bring to the boil. Cover, lower the heat and cook for 15–20 minutes, or until the potatoes are tender.

Finally, add the coconut milk and fresh coriander. Stir and heat through.

Potato & Pea Curry

This is a Delhi/Uttar Pradesh-style dish. I like to use very small, waxy potatoes, each cut in half. If they are larger, you will have to dice them. The potatoes hold together best if you boil them whole and let them cool at room temperature before you peel and cut them.

We generally serve this curry with Indian flatbreads or puffed-up Pooris (see page 224). Pickles and chutneys are served alongside. This combination is very popular for breakfast in northern India. Sips of hot, milky tea ease the spicy potatoes down nicely **Serves 4**

3 tablespoons olive or rapeseed oil

⅛ teaspoon ground asafoetida

¼ teaspoon whole cumin seeds

450g/1 lb small, waxy potatoes, boiled, cooled, peeled and halved (if larger potatoes are used, cut them into 2-cm/1-inch dice)

285 g/10 oz peas, defrosted if frozen

120 ml/4 fl oz natural yoghurt (Greek would be good here)

1½ teaspoons peeled and finely grated fresh ginger

¾ teaspoon salt

¼–½ teaspoon cayenne pepper (or more if you prefer)

1 tablespoon ground coriander

Pour the oil into a large, preferably non-stick sauté pan and set over a medium–high heat. When hot, put in the asafoetida and cumin seeds. Ten seconds later, add the potatoes. Stir and fry until the potatoes have browned lightly.

Now put in the peas, 3 tablespoons of the yoghurt, the ginger, salt and cayenne pepper. Stir and cook until the yoghurt has been absorbed. Add another 3 tablespoons yoghurt and the coriander. Stir and cook until the yoghurt is absorbed again. Add the remaining yoghurt. Stir and cook for 1 minute. If using frozen peas, the dish is now done. If using fresh peas, add 3 tablespoons water, cover, lower the heat and cook very gently for 6–8 minutes, or until the peas are tender.

Potatoes with Cumin & Mustard Seeds

We eat these potatoes with our Indian meals, but also with our eggs on Sundays and our Western roasts and grills. They are versatile and good **Serves 3–4**

675 g/1½ lb waxy potatoes, boiled until just done, cooled thoroughly and peeled

4 tablespoons olive or rapeseed oil

½ teaspoon whole cumin seeds

½ teaspoon whole brown or yellow mustard seeds

1 teaspoon fine slivers of peeled fresh ginger (see page 265)

½ teaspoon salt, or to taste

¼ teaspoon crushed red pepper flakes (or more if desired)

freshly ground black pepper

Cut the potatoes into small dice.

Pour the oil into a frying pan and set over a medium–high heat. When hot, put in the cumin and mustard seeds. As soon as the mustard seeds begin to pop, a matter of seconds, put in the ginger. Stir twice and add the potatoes. Sprinkle the salt, pepper flakes and black pepper over the top. Now stir and fry for 4–5 minutes. The potatoes should get lightly browned and all the spices should be well mixed. Check for salt, adding more if necessary.

Spinach with Garlic & Cumin
Here is a quick stir-fry that can be served with most Indian meals **Serves 4**

675 g/1½ lb spinach

3 tablespoons olive or
  rapeseed oil

1 teaspoon whole cumin seeds

2 cloves garlic, peeled and cut
  into long slivers

½ teaspoon salt

⅛ teaspoon cayenne pepper

Wash the spinach well and chop it coarsely. Leave to drain in a colander.

Pour the oil into a wok or a large pan and set over a medium–high heat. When hot, put in the cumin. When it sizzles, add the garlic. Stir until the garlic slivers turn golden. Add the spinach, stir and cover the pan. When the spinach has wilted completely, remove the lid and add the salt and cayenne pepper. Stir and cook over a high heat, uncovered, until most of the liquid has boiled away.

Sweet & Sour Butternut Squash or Pumpkin

Although this sounds oriental, it belongs to a category of Bangladeshi foods known as *bharats*. Part relish and part vegetable, they add extra flavour to a meal. We are beginning to find peeled and seeded butternut squash in our supermarkets now, making this dish a snap to prepare. Those who cannot find it will need to use a peeler to get the skin off. I like to use mustard oil in the recipe as it gives a very Bengali taste to the dish. If you have never used it, this might be a good time to try. Otherwise, use olive oil. Serve with any type of pork dish, and at vegetarian meals with other vegetables, dal and Pooris (see page 224) **Serves 4–5**

3 tablespoons mustard or olive oil

generous pinch of ground asafoetida

½ teaspoon whole brown or yellow mustard seeds

560 g/1¼ lb peeled and seeded butternut squash or pumpkin, cut into 2.5-cm/1-inch chunks (for instructions see page 267)

¾–1 teaspoon salt

1½ teaspoons caster sugar

⅛–¼ teaspoon cayenne pepper

1 tablespoon natural yoghurt

2 tablespoons chopped fresh coriander

Pour the oil into a frying pan and set over a medium heat. When hot, put in the asafoetida and mustard seeds. As soon as the seeds start to pop, a matter of seconds, put in the squash or pumpkin. Stir and fry for about 3 minutes, or until the pieces just start to brown. Add 50 ml/2 fl oz water, cover, lower the heat and cook for about 10 minutes, or until the squash or pumpkin is tender.

Put in the salt, sugar, cayenne pepper and yoghurt. Stir and cook, uncovered, over a medium heat, until the yoghurt is no longer visible. Put in the fresh coriander and stir a few times.

Quick Sweet & Sour Gujarati Tomato Curry

Here is a dish that takes about 10 minutes to prepare. It is ideally made when tomatoes are in season, but even second-rate, out-of-season tomatoes are given new life by this very Gujarati mixture of seasonings. Serve with rice, a bean or split-pea dish, vegetables and relishes. I also love it with Prawn Biryani and Spinach with Garlic & Cumin (see pages 210 and 169). Grilled pork chops or chicken pieces slathered with this curry are also marvellous combinations

Serves 4–6

3 tablespoons olive or
    rapeseed oil

⅛ teaspoon ground asafoetida

1 teaspoon whole black or
    yellow mustard seeds

1 teaspoon whole cumin seeds

900 g/2 lb medium tomatoes,
    quartered

1 teaspoon salt

¼ teaspoon ground turmeric

¼–½ teaspoon cayenne pepper

2 teaspoons dark brown sugar

1 teaspoon peeled and finely
    grated fresh ginger

Pour the oil into a frying pan and set over a medium–high heat. When hot, put in the asafoetida, mustard seeds and cumin seeds in that order. As soon as the mustard seeds begin to pop, a matter of seconds, put in the tomatoes. Stir once or twice and add the salt, turmeric and cayenne pepper. Stir and add 3 tablespoons water. Bring to the boil. Cover and cook over a medium–high heat for 5 minutes.

Stir the tomatoes, then add the sugar and ginger. Taste and correct the balance of seasonings if necessary. Cover and cook for another 2–3 minutes.

Tomato & Onion Curry

I make this curry throughout the summer, whenever tomatoes overrun the vegetable garden, and then freeze some to last me through the winter. Serve as a vegetarian curry at an Indian meal, or as a gloppy, spicy sauce to ladle over hamburgers, grilled fish and baked or boiled potatoes **Serves 6 (makes about 1.2 litres/40 fl oz)**

1.35 kg/3 lb tomatoes, chopped

salt

3 tablespoons olive or rapeseed oil

generous pinch of ground asafoetida

2 teaspoons skinned urad dal or yellow split peas

2 teaspoons whole brown or yellow mustard seeds

3 whole hot, dried red chillies

15 fresh curry leaves or 6 fresh basil leaves, torn

560 g/1¼ lb onions, peeled and chopped

3 cloves garlic, peeled and finely chopped

2.5-cm/1-inch piece of fresh ginger, peeled and finely chopped

Put the tomatoes and 1½ teaspoons salt in a bowl. Mix and set aside until the tomatoes give off some liquid.

Pour the oil into a wide, heavy pan and set over a medium–high heat. When hot, put in the asafoetida, urad dal and mustard seeds. As soon as the seeds begin to pop, a matter of seconds, put in the chillies, and a few seconds later add the curry leaves and onions. Stir and fry for about 10 minutes, or until the onions are translucent, reducing the heat if necessary so that they do not brown. Add the garlic and ginger and stir for a minute.

Add the tomatoes and their liquid and bring to the boil. Reduce the heat to medium and simmer vigorously for 35–40 minutes, or until the sauce has thickened to a gloppy consistency. Check for salt. You might need to add up to ½ teaspoon more.

Remove the whole chillies and serve hot or at room temperature, as preferred.

South Indian Mixed Vegetable Curry

Known as a vegetable kurma in the Tamil Nadu region, vegetables are diced and parboiled – two vegetables or ten, whatever is in season – drained and then dressed with a coconut–yoghurt mixture seasoned with spices. All vegetables are fair game – aubergines, courgettes, marrows, peas, carrots, potatoes, cauliflower, pumpkin. Many Asian shops sell grated fresh coconut in frozen form, but unsweetened, desiccated coconut can be used instead (see page 263). In southern India this dish is generally eaten at room temperature (balmy) with rice and legumes, but I often serve it in the summer, when my garden is at its most productive, almost as a salad/vegetable dish that accompanies Indian or Western meats   **Serves 4**

2 medium carrots (about 180 g/6 oz), peeled and cut into 1-cm/½–inch dice

115 g/4 oz green beans (flat or round), cut into 1-cm/½-inch pieces

140 g/5 oz peas, defrosted if frozen

salt

3 tablespoons grated fresh coconut (see above)

6 tablespoons natural yoghurt

¼–½ teaspoon cayenne pepper

2 tablespoons olive or rapeseed oil

½ teaspoon whole brown mustard seeds

¼ teaspoon skinned urad dal or yellow split peas

1 whole dried, hot red chilli

10–15 fresh curry leaves or 6 fresh basil leaves, torn

Bring 250 ml/8 fl oz water to the boil in a small pan. When boiling, add ½ teaspoon salt and the carrots, beans and peas. Boil for about 3–4 minutes, or until the vegetables are just tender. Drain and put in a bowl.

Combine the coconut, yoghurt, cayenne pepper and ½ teaspoon salt, stirring well to make a sauce. Pour this over the vegetables but do not mix yet.

Pour the oil into a small frying pan and set over a medium–high heat. When hot, put in the mustard seeds, urad dal and chilli. As soon as the seeds begin to pop, a matter of seconds, put in the curry leaves, then pour the mixture over the coconut–yoghurt dressing. Now mix the vegetables gently with the dressing and spices, and serve warm or at room temperature.

Dal – Dried Beans, Legumes & Split Peas

Indians are hard put to find an all-encompassing English name for what they eat every day in some form – *dal*. Many just call it 'lentils' and hope for the best. As a result, you will find poppadoms labelled 'lentil wafers', even though they are made from various split-pea flours. For Westerners, though, lentils conjure up specific images of red, green, brown and French lentils; dried beans are never included under that name, nor are chickpeas or split peas. In India all these things are dals.

I have decided to use the word 'dal' throughout this book because nothing else will really do. To pronounce the word correctly, just remember that the 'a' is a long one, as in 'calm' and that the 'd' is soft. Technically, because the word comes from *dalna* (to split), *dal* really means 'split peas'. But the word has come to stand for the whole family of dried beans and dried peas, both split and whole, skinned and unskinned.

For most Indians, dal is a major source of protein, combined as it often is at the table with a grain (usually rice or flatbreads) and either natural yoghurt set at home or a yoghurt relish. The mould of a traditional Indian repast was cast in ancient times and is used to this day. When I was growing up, our family lunch generally contained no meat (unless it was a holiday). What we had was rice or chapatis, a dal, two vegetables, a salad and some yoghurt.

We pretty much ate what all of India was eating. The rice or chapatis were the constant. Everything else was varied on a daily basis.

Indians eat many different dals, and we cook them in many different ways: the spicing can be varied; you might have a particular dal one day and another the next, or dals may be mixed; you could roast a split-pea dal before cooking it; you could cook a dal with meat, fish or a vegetable; you could make a dish with a dal flour. You can actually go for months and not eat the same dal dish twice.

Some of the dals are of Indian origin. *Moong dal* (also called mung beans, and used in eastern Asia to make beansprouts) and the slightly glutinous *urad dal* both have an ancient history in India. Chickpeas and red lentils came via the Middle East, but were early arrivals. India was growing chickpeas in 2500 BC. *Toor dal* (pigeon peas) might have come from Africa, but could also have developed simultaneously in India.

Many of the whole beans, such as kidney beans in various hues, came from the New World with conquering colonialists around the 16th century. The colonialists were eventually thrown out, but India kept the beans, adding them to its already vast collection of dals.

If you were to walk into an Indian dal shop, you would find an outstanding variety. First of all, there are the whole beans and peas: kidney beans large and small, black-eyed peas, red lentils (*sabut masoor*), *urad dal*, *moong* beans, chickpeas (green, black, beige, large and small) and many more. Then you have most of them in their split forms with and without skin. You also have flours made with nearly all of them, the most popular being the very nutritious chickpea flour (gram flour).

Almost no South Asian home is without chickpea flour. It is used to make fritters, dumplings and a whole family of snack foods. It is also used to thicken soupy stews, and added to yoghurt sauces when they are being heated to prevent curdling.

I remember my mother making fritters on cool monsoon days. She would make a chickpea flour batter, dip thinly sliced potatoes and cauliflower florets and whole chillies in it, then deep-fry them all. We would eat these with a green chutney. I try to do the same for my grandchildren. On cold winter days I make my own thick batter (of a dropping consistency) and dip cut-up prawns and onions in it. I remove one heaped teaspoon at a time and drop it into hot oil, frying the fritters until they are a rich, reddish-gold colour. We all sit by the fire and devour them. (See Prawn & Onion Fritters, page 27.)

The normal everyday dal is wet and somewhat soupy – its final texture is a personal decision, and ranges from the very thin to the very thick. (In India, there is a saying that when guests drop in, you just add more water to the dal!) Those eating it with rice take their rice first and then ladle some of the dal over it and some to the side, so it can be eaten in two ways – mixed with the rice or combined with the vegetables or yoghurt or pickles. When eating it with flatbreads, it is ladled into small metal bowls known as *katoris*. This way it is easier to scoop it up with the breads. There are exceptions, of course. Black beans (*kali dal*) are generally cooked to be quite thick and are spooned directly on to the plate.

Most dals start out by being washed and then boiled in water until they are tender. They are quite bland at this stage. The transformation comes at the end when oil or ghee is heated in a small pan, spices and seasonings dropped into it until they sizzle and then all this is poured over the boiled dal.

The fresher the dal, the faster it cooks. If you have old dried beans, peas or lentils that have been sitting around for years, it's probably a good idea to throw them away, or be prepared to cook them for hours and hours. Dals are best eaten within a year of being picked and dried. Two-year-old dals are still fine, but may require longer cooking.

Black-eyed Beans with Butternut Squash

Indians combine dried beans and peas with almost any vegetable. Here I use either pumpkin or butternut squash, which gives a mellow sweetness to the dish. In India this would be eaten with wholemeal flatbreads, yoghurt relishes, salads and pickles. For a Western meal, the beans may be served with a sliced baguette as a first course, or with roast pork or lamb   **Serves 6**

340 g/12 oz dried black-eyed beans

3 tablespoons olive or rapeseed oil

½ teaspoon whole cumin seeds

½ teaspoon whole fennel seeds

1 medium onion, peeled and chopped

3 cloves garlic, peeled and finely chopped

½ teaspoon peeled and finely chopped fresh ginger

1 fresh hot green chilli, chopped

4 tablespoons tomato passata (see page 268)

1½ teaspoons salt

⅛–¼ teaspoon cayenne pepper

340 g/12 oz peeled and seeded butternut squash or pumpkin, cut into 2.5-cm/1-inch pieces (see page 267)

Soak the black–eyed beans overnight in water that covers them well. Drain.

Pour the oil into a large, heavy pan and set over a medium–high heat. When hot, put in the cumin and fennel seeds. Let them sizzle for 10 seconds, then add the onion. Stir and fry until it browns at the edges. Add the garlic, ginger and chilli. Stir for 1 minute. Add the tomato passata. Stir for 1 minute. Now put in the beans, salt, cayenne pepper, squash and 1.12 litres/36 fl oz water. Bring to the boil. Cover partially, lower the heat and cook for about 1 hour, or until the beans are tender.

Black Beans

Indian black beans (sold as *sabut ma* or whole urad with skin) are different from those eaten in much of the Caribbean, Mexico and Central America. The Indian ones are actually a very, very dark shade of green, but manage to look black. The Central American variety (*frijoles negros*) is actually black. However, one may be substituted for the other, even though each has a somewhat different taste and texture. Below is a recipe for dried black beans (Indian or Central American) cooked in a simple north-west Indian way. These beans are normally eaten with wholemeal flatbreads, vegetables (such as aubergines) and yoghurt relishes. They may also be served with rice. Wholemeal pita bread may be substituted for the Indian flatbreads **Serves 6**

400 g/14 oz black beans, picked over and washed

2 teaspoons salt, or to taste

2 teaspoons peeled and very finely grated fresh ginger

2 cloves garlic, peeled and crushed

4 tablespoons chopped fresh coriander

6 tablespoons tomato purée

175 ml/6 fl oz single cream

60 g/2 oz unsalted butter

Soak the beans overnight in water that covers them generously. Drain them the next day and put them in a heavy pan along with 1.6 litres/52 fl oz water. Bring to the boil. Cover partially, lower the heat and simmer very gently for 1½–2 hours, or until the beans are tender. (Older beans might take longer to cook.)

Add the salt, ginger, garlic, coriander and tomato purée. Stir to mix well and continue to cook over a low heat for another 30 minutes. Add the cream and stir in. Just before serving, bring the beans back to a simmer. Add the butter and stir it in.

Canned Beans with Indian Spices
Sometimes when I am in a rush but longing for a dal, I take the simple way out and use canned beans – black, white haricot, cannellini, or any other beans I like. Today we can get organic canned beans of excellent quality, and it takes barely 15 minutes to cook them. Even the liquid in the can tastes good, so I do not have to throw it away. Serve these beans with rice or Indian flatbreads **Serves 2–3**

2 tablespoons olive or rapeseed oil

generous pinch of ground asafoetida

¼ teaspoon whole cumin seeds

½ medium onion, peeled and sliced into fine half-rings

4 cherry tomatoes, quartered

⅛–¼ teaspoon cayenne pepper

¼ teaspoon ground turmeric

1 x 425-g/15-oz can black, white haricot, cannellini, or any other beans, preferably organic

½ teaspoon salt, or as needed

Pour the oil into a small pan and set over a medium–high heat. When hot, put in the asafoetida and cumin seeds. Let the seeds sizzle for 5 seconds. Add the onion and reduce the heat to medium. Stir and cook until it has browned a bit. Add the tomatoes and stir a few times. Now add the cayenne pepper and turmeric. Stir once or twice, then add the contents of the can (beans and liquid if organic, otherwise just the beans and the same amount of water as liquid), as well as 4 tablespoons water. Stir and bring to a simmer. Cover, lower the heat and simmer gently for 10 minutes. Taste and add as much salt as needed.

Chickpeas with Mushrooms

I use cremini mushrooms here as they are very firm, but ordinary white mushrooms will do. If you want the dish to be hotter, you can add one to two teaspoons finely chopped fresh, hot green chillies towards the end of the cooking, as many Indians do. This dish may be served at a meal, but also makes a wonderful filling for a 'wrap' if rolled inside any flatbread. Thinly sliced onions, fresh coriander and chopped tomatoes may be rolled inside as well. If preferred, simply add one of my chutneys or a good-quality shop-bought salsa instead **Serves 4**

4 tablespoons olive or rapeseed oil

½ teaspoon whole cumin seeds

1 x 5-cm/2-inch cinnamon stick

½ medium red onion, peeled and finely chopped

2 teaspoons peeled and finely grated fresh ginger

1 large clove garlic, peeled and crushed

10 medium mushrooms (about 225 g/8 oz), cut through the stalk into slices 7 mm/¼ inch thick

2 teaspoons ground coriander

½ teaspoon ground cumin

¼ teaspoon ground turmeric

½ teaspoon cayenne pepper

½ medium tomato, chopped

350 g/12½ oz cooked, drained chickpeas, liquid reserved if organic

¾–1 teaspoon salt, or to taste

Pour the oil into a wide pan and set over a medium–high heat. When hot, put in the cumin seeds and cinnamon. Let the spices sizzle for a few seconds, then add the onion. Stir and fry until the edges brown a bit. Add the ginger and garlic and stir once or twice. Add the mushrooms. Stir until they are softened. Add the coriander, cumin, turmeric and cayenne pepper. Stir a few times. Add the tomato and 120 ml/4 fl oz of either the chickpea liquid (if organic) or water. Cover, lower the heat and cook for 10 minutes.

Add the chickpeas, salt and another 250 ml/8 fl oz of the organic chickpea liquid or water or a mixture of the two. Bring to a simmer. Cover, lower the heat and cook gently for 15–20 minutes, stirring now and then.

Spicy Chickpeas with Potatoes

Here is an everyday dish with a fair number of ingredients, but you can do some of the chopping in a food processor. Once you have them all prepared and assembled, the rest is fairly easy. Serve with Indian or Middle Eastern breads (you can even roll up the chickpeas inside them), with Yoghurt Sambol with Tomato & Shallot (see page 243) on the side. For dinner, add meat and a vegetable **Serves 6**

2 tablespoons ground coriander

2 teaspoons ground cumin

½ teaspoon cayenne pepper

½ teaspoon ground turmeric

4 tablespoons olive or rapeseed oil

70 g/2½ oz peeled and finely chopped red onions or shallots

2 teaspoons peeled and finely grated fresh ginger

2 cloves garlic, peeled and crushed

140 g/5 oz finely chopped tomato

2 x 400-g/14-oz cans organic chickpeas, drained and liquid reserved

2 medium potatoes (140–180 g/ 5–6 oz), peeled and cut into 2-cm/¾-inch dice

1 teaspoon salt

Combine the coriander, cumin, cayenne pepper, turmeric and 3 tablespoons water in a small bowl. Mix well.

Pour the oil into a medium pan and set over a medium heat. When hot, put in the onions. Stir and fry for 3–4 minutes, or until lightly browned. Add the ginger and garlic. Stir for 1 minute. Put in the spice mixture from the bowl. Stir for a few seconds. Add the tomato. Stir and cook for about 3 minutes, or until the tomato has softened.

Add the chickpeas and 350 ml/12 fl oz of their liquid, adding extra water if needed to make the right amount. Now add the potatoes and salt. Bring to the boil. Cover, lower the heat and simmer gently until the potatoes are tender, about 15–20 minutes.

Chickpeas in a Sauce

There was a time when canned chickpeas came in such a tinny-tasting liquid that they not only needed draining but rinsing as well. The liquid was unusable. Lately, I have found canned organic chickpeas that are in a lovely natural liquid, quite similar to what I get when I boil my own. This is a giant leap indeed. Look for them. Serve with Indian flatbreads or rice. An aubergine dish, greens and relishes would complete the meal. Meats can always be added if you wish **Serves 4**

3 tablespoons olive or rapeseed oil

¾ teaspoon whole cumin seeds

140 g/5 oz peeled and finely chopped onions

1 teaspoon peeled and finely grated fresh ginger

¾ teaspoon ground coriander

¼–½ teaspoon cayenne pepper

¼ teaspoon ground turmeric

140 g/5 oz finely chopped tomato

1 teaspoon salt

350 g/12½ oz cooked, drained chickpeas, liquid reserved if organic

½ teaspoon garam masala, preferably home-made (see page 264), but shop-bought will do

1 teaspoon lemon juice

Pour the oil into a frying pan and set over a medium heat. When hot, put in the cumin seeds. After 10 seconds, put in the onions. Stir and fry until the onions brown at the edges. Add the ginger and stir once. Add the coriander, cayenne pepper and turmeric and stir once. Put in the tomato and stir for 1 minute. Now add 250 ml/8 fl oz water and the salt. Bring to the boil. Cover, lower the heat and simmer for 10 minutes.

Add the chickpeas and 250 ml/8 fl oz of their liquid, or water if the liquid is non-organic. Bring to the boil. Cover, lower the heat and cook for 15 minutes. Add the garam masala and lemon juice. Stir and cook, uncovered, over a low heat for another 5 minutes.

Yoghurt Sauce (*Karhi*)

As yoghurt would curdle into unappetising blobs if it were just heated up, it is stabilised first with flour. In India, where there are many vegetarians who know that a bean, a grain and a milk product can make for a balanced meal, it is chickpea flour that is used. Also known as gram flour and *besan*, it is very nutritious and full of nutty flavour. *Karhis* are cooked throughout much of India, with many interesting regional variations. This yoghurt sauce, spicily seasoned and quite scrumptious, is either poured over rice or put into individual bowls and eaten with wholemeal flatbreads. Meats and vegetables are often served on the side **Serves 6**

100 g/3½ oz chickpea flour, sifted

475 ml/16 fl oz natural yoghurt, preferably 'bio'

3 tablespoons olive or rapeseed oil

1½ teaspoons whole cumin seeds

1½ teaspoons whole brown or yellow mustard seeds

1 teaspoon whole fennel seeds

3 whole hot, dried red chillies

½ teaspoon ground turmeric

About 15 fresh curry leaves or 8 fresh basil leaves, torn

1¾ teaspoons salt

Put the flour in a large bowl. Very slowly add 250 ml/8 fl oz water, beating with a whisk as you do so. Keep beating until there are no lumps. Add the yoghurt and beat until the mixture is smooth. Gradually add another 1 litre/32 fl oz water, beating as you go.

Pour the oil into a medium pan and set over a medium–high heat. When hot, put in the cumin, mustard and fennel seeds and the chillies. As soon as the mustard seeds start to pop, a matter of seconds, put in the turmeric and curry leaves. Stir once, then pour in the yoghurt mixture. Stir with a whisk. Reduce the heat to medium. Add the salt. Keep stirring with the whisk until the mixture thickens and starts to bubble. Lower the heat, cover partially and cook for 25 minutes.

Red Lentils with Ginger

Red lentils, sold in Indian shops as skinless *masoor dal* and in some places as Egyptian red lentils, usually come in various shades of salmon pink. They originated in the Middle East, but reached India quite early and are eaten throughout the north of the country. This particular dish may be served with most Indian meals. It also happens to be particularly scrumptious over pasta, such as penne or fusilli **Serves 4–5**

3 cloves garlic, peeled and crushed

1 teaspoon peeled and finely grated fresh ginger

1 tablespoon ground coriander

1 teaspoon ground cumin

¼ teaspoon cayenne pepper

¼ teaspoon ground turmeric

3 tablespoons olive or rapeseed oil

4 tablespoons peeled and chopped onions

140 g/5 oz finely chopped tomatoes

200 g/7 oz red lentils (skinless masoor dal), washed and drained

¾–1 teaspoon salt

3 tablespoons chopped fresh coriander

1 tablespoon unsalted butter (optional)

Combine the garlic, ginger, ground coriander, cumin, cayenne pepper and turmeric in a small bowl and mix.

Pour the oil into a wide, medium pan and set over a medium heat. When hot, put in the onions. Stir and fry until they turn golden at the edges. Add the spice mixture from the bowl. Stir for 1 minute. Add the tomatoes. Stir and cook, scraping the bottom, until the tomatoes have softened.

Now put in the lentils, 800 ml/28 fl oz water and the salt. Bring to the boil. Cover partially, lower the heat and cook for 45 minutes. Stir well and cook uncovered for another 5 minutes. Stir in the fresh coriander and butter (if using) just before serving.

Bangladeshi Red Lentils

Here is an everyday dal to be served with rice, vegetables and curries. (In Bangladesh the curry would often be made with fish.) **Serves 4–5**

200 g/7 oz red lentils (skinless masoor dal), washed and drained

¼ teaspoon ground turmeric

1 medium onion, peeled and one half finely chopped, the other sliced into fine half-rings

¾–1 teaspoon salt

3 tablespoons olive or rapeseed oil or ghee

2 cloves garlic, peeled and cut into thin slices

2–3 hot, dried red chillies, each broken in half

Put the lentils, turmeric and chopped onion in a medium pan with 800 ml/28 fl oz water. Bring to the boil. Cover partially, lower the heat and cook for 45 minutes, or until the lentils are very tender. Add the salt and mix in.

Pour the oil into a small frying pan set over a medium heat. When hot, put in the sliced onions and stir a few times. Add the garlic and chillies. Stir and fry until the onion and garlic turn a rich golden-red. Pour the contents of the frying pan into the lentils. Stir to mix.

Goan-style Dal Curry

This delicious curry can also be made with *moong dal* (skinned and split mung beans) or mixed half and half with them. Serve with rice and some fish **Serves 4–5**

200 g/7 oz red lentils (skinless masoor dal), washed and drained

½ teaspoon ground turmeric

2 medium tomatoes, peeled and chopped (see page 267)

1½ teaspoons salt

50 g/1¾ oz chopped fresh coriander

½–¾ teaspoon cayenne pepper

2 tablespoons olive or rapeseed oil

½ teaspoon whole brown mustard seeds

½ teaspoon whole cumin seeds

½ medium onion, peeled and chopped

10–15 fresh curry leaves or 6 fresh basil leaves, torn

1 teaspoon peeled and very finely grated fresh ginger

1 large clove garlic, peeled and crushed

Put the lentils and 700 ml/24 fl oz water in a medium pan. Bring to the boil but do not let it boil over. Skim off the froth and add the turmeric. Stir, cover partially, reduce the heat to very low and simmer gently for 40 minutes.

Add the tomatoes, salt, coriander and cayenne pepper. Bring to a simmer. Cover, lower the heat and simmer for 10 minutes. Stir and turn off the heat.

Pour the oil into a small frying pan and set over a medium–high heat. When hot, put in the mustard and cumin seeds. As soon as the mustard seeds begin to pop, a matter of seconds, put in the onion and curry leaves. Stir and fry until the onion starts to brown. Now put in the ginger and garlic. Stir for 1 minute, then empty the contents of the pan into the lentils. Stir to mix.

My Everyday Moong Dal

My family can eat this every single day of the week: it is our soul food. I love this with Plain Basmati Rice (see page 201) and any vegetable I feel like that day. It's also excellent with Lemony Minced Lamb with Mint & Coriander (see page 113) **Serves 4–6**

200 g/7 oz moong dal (skinned and split mung beans), washed and drained

¼ teaspoon ground turmeric

¾ teaspoon salt, or to taste

2 tablespoons olive oil or ghee

⅛ teaspoon ground asafoetida

½ teaspoon whole cumin seeds

1–2 whole hot, dried red chillies

1 medium shallot, peeled and cut into fine slivers

Put the moong dal in a medium pan and add 800 ml/28 fl oz water. Bring to the boil. Skim off the white froth and add the turmeric. Stir to mix. Cover partially, reduce the heat to a gentle simmer and cook for 45 minutes. Add the salt and stir to mix. Turn off the heat.

Pour the oil into a small frying pan and set over a medium–high heat. When hot, quickly add the asafoetida, cumin seeds and chillies in that order. As soon as the chillies darken, a matter of seconds, put in the shallot. Stir and cook until it browns, then quickly pour the contents of the frying pan over the cooked dal. Stir to mix.

Roasted Moong Dal with Mustard Greens (*Bhaja Moong Dal*)

This is a Bengali speciality that requires the moong dal (skinned and split mung beans) to be lightly roasted first. Then, when the dal is almost done, quick-cooking greens are added to make it more nourishing. There are several tiny steps required here, but each is simplicity itself. I find that most split peas and beans are so clean these days that they need no picking over, but you do need to rinse them off. In this recipe the rinsing is done after the roasting for obvious reasons.

For many peasants, such a dal, served with rice and perhaps followed by a yoghurt dessert, makes for a rich, ample meal. You may add a fish dish   **Serves 4–6**

180 g/6 oz skinned and split moong dal

¼ teaspoon ground turmeric

85 g/3 oz mustard greens, or other tender greens, such as spinach or Swiss chard, well chopped

1¼ teaspoons salt

1½ tablespoons extra virgin olive oil

½ teaspoon whole brown or yellow mustard seeds

½ teaspoon whole cumin seeds

¼ teaspoon whole nigella seeds (kalonji)

¼ teaspoon whole fennel seeds

2 whole hot, dried red chillies

Put the unwashed dal in a medium pan and set over a medium heat. Shake or stir until some of the grains turn a little brown. Now pour cold water into the pan, stir the grains and pour the water out. Rinse one more time.

Drain the dal well, then return to the pan and add 1 litre/ 32 fl oz fresh water. Add the turmeric and bring to the boil (do not allow to boil over). Cover partially, lower the heat and cook for 30 minutes.

Add the greens and salt to the dal. Stir and cook, partially covered, for another 20 minutes, stirring now and then.

Heat the oil in a small frying pan. When hot, put in all the seeds and the chillies in the order listed. As soon as the mustard seeds begin to pop, a matter of seconds, pour the contents of the pan over the cooked dal and cover it for a few minutes to allow the aromas to be absorbed. Stir before serving.

Arhar Dal with Tomato & Onion

The Indian split peas *arhar dal* and *toor* (or *toovar*) *dal* are closely related. Both are the skinned and split descendants of the pigeon pea. Arhar, the north Indian version, is mild in flavour, whereas *toor*, used in west and south India, tends to be darker and earthier. Use whichever you can find. If you cannot find either, use yellow split peas. Serve with rice or Indian flatbreads. Add a vegetable and relishes to complete the meal. Non-vegetarians could add meat or fish, if they like **Serves 4–6**

210 g/7¼ oz arhar/toor dal, or yellow split peas, washed and drained

½ teaspoon ground turmeric

1½ teaspoons salt

¼–¾ teaspoon cayenne pepper

3 tablespoons olive or rapeseed oil or ghee

½ teaspoon whole cumin seeds

½ teaspoon whole brown mustard seeds

15–20 fresh curry leaves or 10 fresh basil leaves, torn

1 medium onion, peeled and chopped

2 medium tomatoes, chopped

Put the dal and 1.12 litres/36 fl oz water in a medium pan. Bring to the boil and skim off the froth that rises to the top. Lower the heat and add the turmeric. Stir, cover partially and simmer gently for 1 hour.

Add the salt and cayenne pepper to the dal. Stir, cover partially again and simmer gently for about 10 minutes, or until you finish the next step.

Pour the oil into a medium frying pan over a medium heat. When it is very hot, put in the cumin and mustard seeds. As soon as the mustard seeds pop, a matter of seconds, add the curry leaves and onion. Stir and fry until the onion has softened a bit and is beginning to brown at the edges. Add the tomatoes and stir over a medium–low heat until they have also softened a bit, about 2 minutes. Pour the contents of the frying pan into the dal and stir through.

Toor Dal with Corn

I have eaten this slightly sweet and sour dish only in Gujarat, and how good it was too. It isn't corn kernels that are cooked in the dal, but the cob itself, lopped into reasonably sized rounds. The woody part of the cob flavours the dal in mysterious ways. You just cannot eat these cob pieces with cutlery: hands are required. If you cannot find *toor dal* (also labelled *toovar dal* or the similar *arhar dal*), use any other split peas that you can find easily, such as red lentils or yellow split peas. Just remember that red lentils cook faster than *toor dal*. This dal is put into individual serving bowls and served with rice or Indian flatbreads. A selection of other vegetables and relishes is also included in vegetarian meals. Non-vegetarians might add fish or chicken **Serves 4–5**

210 g/7¼ oz toor dal or similar (see above), washed and drained

¼ teaspoon ground turmeric

1 fresh corn cob, cut crossways into 2.5-cm/1-inch pieces (or as many pieces as there are diners)

1¼ teaspoons salt

¼–¾ teaspoon cayenne pepper

1 tablespoon lemon juice

2 teaspoons caster sugar

2 tablespoons olive or rapeseed oil or ghee

⅛ teaspoon ground asafoetida

3 cloves

½ teaspoon whole cumin seeds

½ teaspoon whole brown mustard seeds

2 whole hot, dried red chillies

Put the dal and 1 litre/32 fl oz water in a medium pan. Bring to the boil and skim off the froth that rises to the top. Lower the heat and add the turmeric. Stir, cover partially and simmer gently for 1 hour.

Add the corn, salt, cayenne pepper, lemon juice and sugar to the pan. Stir, cover partially again and simmer gently for 10 minutes.

Heat the oil in a small frying pan. When it is very hot, put in the asafoetida, cloves, cumin and mustard seeds, and chillies. As soon as the mustard seeds pop, a matter of seconds, pour the contents of the frying pan into the dal. Stir and serve.

Green Lentils with Green Beans & Fresh Coriander

For vegetarians, these refreshing lentils, accompanied perhaps by Yoghurt Relish with Okra (see page 248) and a bread, either Indian or crusty Western, could make an entire meal. For non-vegetarians, meat or fish curries may be added **Serves 4–6**

250 g/9 oz green lentils

1 teaspoon salt

¼ teaspoon cayenne pepper

115 g/4 oz green beans, cut into 2-cm/¾-inch segments

60 g/2 oz finely chopped fresh coriander

3 tablespoons olive or rapeseed oil

⅛ teaspoon ground asafoetida

½ teaspoon whole cumin seeds

1 medium shallot, peeled and cut into fine slivers

lemon wedges (optional)

Put the lentils and 950 ml/34 fl oz water in a medium pan and bring to the boil. Cover partially, lower the heat and simmer very gently for 20 minutes. Add the salt, cayenne pepper, green beans and coriander. Stir to mix and bring to the boil again. Cover partially and simmer very gently for another 20 minutes. Turn off the heat.

Pour the oil into a small frying pan and set over a medium–high heat. When hot, put in the asafoetida and cumin. Let the seeds sizzle for 10 seconds. Add the shallot. Stir and fry over a medium heat until it turns reddish. Now pour the entire contents of the frying pan into the pan with the lentils. Stir to mix. Offer with lemon wedges at the table, if you wish.

Rice & Other Grains

In much of South Asia, grains form the heart of a meal. While Westerners might say, 'I feel like roast lamb today – what should I have with it?' most South Asians will just assume that some form of rice, bread or noodles will be part of their meal, depending upon what tradition they were born into. The only question for them would be, 'What do I want to complement my grain-based staple with today?'

Let us look at a village in Punjab. This could be Punjab in the eastern section of Pakistan, or Punjab in the north-western section of India. As both Punjabs were once a single state in pre-Independence India, their food is fairly similar. The staple would be wholemeal breads made in the tandoor or, for breakfast, wholemeal parathas (griddle breads) made on cast-iron griddles. All families would eat the breads with a dal, pickles, perhaps a vegetable and yoghurt. In Pakistan they might substitute a meat kebab or curry for the vegetable. On special occasions they would all make a rice pilaf.

Now take a village in south India, Bangladesh or Sri Lanka, where the staple is rice. A mound of rice would be cooked for a family. It would be very plain. It would also be unsalted, ready to absorb flavours from its spicy accompaniments. These might (in Bangladesh, Sri Lanka and some coastal regions of south India) include a fish curry, and certainly a dal and yoghurt for all the south Indian vegetarians.

On special occasions there would be some flatbreads as well, made out of rice flour or wheat flour. Breakfasts in south India and Sri Lanka might have rice flour noodles served with cardamom-flavoured fresh coconut milk, ground rice pancakes served with coconut chutney or a dal, or other savoury, rice-based cakes. Fine rice noodles, freshly made by pushing rice dough through a mould and then steaming the nest that is formed, are very common and eaten at breakfast, lunch and dinner. At dinner these might even be served with a fish curry. While it is not easy to make rice noodles at home unless you are well practised, it is very simple to buy dried, East Asian rice sticks and to reconstitute them in water (see page 219).

Wheat is the basis of more than just flatbreads. A coarse semolina is used throughout south Asia to make sweet halvas and savoury pilafs. There is a Semolina Pilaf with Peas on page 206. In Punjab I have even had pilafs made out of bulgar wheat (see page 218).

In Delhi, my home town, our real staple was wheat, which we ate in the form of small, delicate chapatis (wholemeal flatbreads) made out of wholemeal flour. But we also ate rice (basmati) at lunchtime. All the meats, vegetables, dals and relishes were first offered with unsalted Plain Basmati Rice (see page 201), and then with the Chapatis (see page 222). On Sundays we often had a rich meat pilaf for lunch, with several vegetables and relishes on the side. On many occasions there were meatballs as well.

Rice can be cooked with almost anything – just some spices and seasonings, fresh seasonal peas, dal, meat, tomato, nuts and dried fruit, prawns, coconut – whatever your fancy desires. You will find many such recipes in this chapter.

While South Asians might be addicted to their breads or their rice, all of you cooking from this book can mix and match at will. Do whatever is easy and convenient. If you don't feel up to making flatbreads or rice, eat your curry with a pita bread, a French baguette, a corn tortilla or a 'selice'. What is a 'selice'? In the inner cities of India and Pakistan you will find many a citizen sitting at an outdoor table at a cheap restaurant, scooping up his fiery curry with a 'selice' of bread. Yes, that is a slice from a loaf of bread!

Plain Basmati Rice
Basmati rice is easy to cook if you follow these simple directions: buy good-quality rice where the grains are unbroken and the rice has a pronounced basmati perfume; wash, soak and drain the rice; cook it without heavy-handed stirring, as the grains can break easily. This could be an everyday rice when served with a simple dal, vegetable and relish, or a party rice if served with a fish or meat curry **Serves 6**

a 475-ml/16-fl oz measure of basmati rice

Put the rice in a bowl. Cover with cold water and stir gently. Pour out the dirty water. Do this 4 or 5 times. Now cover well with fresh water and leave to soak for 30 minutes (longer will not hurt). Drain and leave in a sieve set over a bowl to drain further.

Put the drained rice in a heavy pan that has a tight-fitting lid. Add 650 ml/22 fl oz water and bring to the boil. Cover tightly, reduce the heat to very, very low and simmer gently for 25 minutes.

When ready to serve, remove the rice with a slotted spoon, breaking up the lumps gently with the back of the spoon.

Yellow Basmati Rice with Sesame Seeds

Not only does this rice look colourful and taste delicious, but the turmeric acts like an antiseptic inside the body, and the sesame seeds add a good deal of nutrition. You can almost eat this rice by itself. Add a dal, perhaps an aubergine dish and a yoghurt relish, and you have a fine vegetarian meal. Or serve with kebabs of any sort and a salad for a light, non-vegetarian meal **Serves 4–6**

a 475-ml/16-fl oz measure of basmati rice

2 tablespoons olive or rapeseed oil

1 whole dried, hot red chilli

1 teaspoon skinned urad dal or yellow split peas

1 teaspoon whole brown or yellow mustard seeds

1 tablespoon sesame seeds

½ teaspoon ground turmeric

1 teaspoon salt (optional)

Put the rice in a bowl. Cover with cold water and stir gently. Pour out the dirty water. Do this 4 or 5 times. Now cover well with fresh water and leave to soak for 30 minutes (longer will not hurt). Drain and leave in a sieve set over a bowl to drain further.

Pour the oil into a heavy-based medium pan that has a tight-fitting lid and set over a medium–high heat. When hot, put in the chilli, urad dal, mustard seeds and sesame seeds. As soon as the dal turns reddish and the mustard seeds begin to pop, add the drained rice, turmeric and salt (if using). Lower the heat to medium. Stir very gently and sauté for 1 minute. Add 600 ml/20 fl oz water and bring to the boil. Cover tightly, reduce the heat to very, very low and simmer gently for 25 minutes.

When ready to serve, remove the rice with a slotted spoon, breaking up the lumps gently with the back of the spoon.

Rice Pilaf with Almonds & Sultanas

Pilafs may be served at everyday meals, but are generally grand enough for entertaining as well. If you like, you could add a generous pinch of saffron threads to the rice just before you cover it and let it simmer. You could also use chicken stock instead of the water **Serves 4–6**

a 450-ml/15-fl oz measure of basmati rice

3 tablespoons olive or rapeseed oil or ghee

1 x 5-cm/2-inch cinnamon stick

½ medium onion, peeled and sliced into fine half-rings

2 tablespoons slivered blanched almonds

2 tablespoons sultanas

1 teaspoon salt

Put the rice in a bowl. Cover with cold water and stir gently. Pour out the dirty water. Do this 4 or 5 times. Now cover well with fresh water and leave to soak for 30 minutes (longer will not hurt). Drain and leave in a sieve set over a bowl to drain further.

Pour the oil into a heavy-based medium pan that has a tight-fitting lid and set over a medium–high heat. When hot, put in the cinnamon. Let it sizzle for 10 seconds. Put in the onion. Stir and fry until it starts to brown. Add the almonds. Stir until they are golden. Add the sultanas. Stir until they are plump, just a few seconds.

Add the drained rice and salt. Stir very gently to mix. Add 600 ml/20 fl oz water and bring to the boil. Cover tightly, reduce the heat to very, very low and simmer gently for 25 minutes.

When ready to serve, remove the rice with a slotted spoon, breaking up the lumps gently with the back of the spoon.

Sri Lankan Rice with Fresh Coriander & Lemon Grass

I had this aromatic and festive dish in the museum-like home of batik artist Ena de Silva. Lemon grass is grown on the edge of the more precipitous slopes of Sri Lanka's numerous tea gardens. Some of these plantations are visible from the front patio of Ena's mountain bungalow. Lemon grass keeps insects away, and its long roots hold back the soil. At Ena's the dish was served with dozens of curries and relishes. You may serve this at banquets and family meals alike. It goes well with coconut milk-based curries, such as Kerala-style Chicken Curry (see page 94) **Serves 4–6**

a 475-ml/16-fl oz measure of basmati rice

3 tablespoons olive or rapeseed oil

3 cardamom pods

3 cloves

1 x 5-cm/2-inch cinnamon stick

10 fresh curry leaves or 5 fresh basil leaves, torn

2 cloves garlic, peeled and crushed

2 teaspoons peeled and finely grated fresh ginger

15 cm/6 inches lemon grass, from the bottom of the stalk, cut crossways into 2 pieces

60 g/2 oz finely chopped fresh coriander (only tender stems and leaves)

650 ml/22 fl oz chicken stock

1 teaspoon salt (1½ teaspoons if the stock is unsalted)

Put the rice in a bowl. Cover with cold water and stir gently. Pour out the dirty water. Do this 4 or 5 times. Now cover well with fresh water and leave to soak for 30 minutes (longer will not hurt). Drain and leave in a sieve set over a bowl to drain further.

Pour the oil into a heavy-based medium pan and set over a medium–high heat. When hot, put in the cardamom, cloves and cinnamon. Let them sizzle for 5 seconds. Put in the curry leaves, garlic, ginger and lemon grass. Stir for 1 minute.

Add the drained rice and coriander. Reduce the heat to medium and stir for a minute. Add the stock and salt and bring to the boil. Cover tightly, reduce the heat to very, very low and cook gently for 25 minutes.

When ready to serve, remove the rice with a slotted spoon, breaking up the lumps gently with the back of the spoon.

Tomato Pullao

Here is a delicious pilaf that may be served with most Indian meals **Serves 6**

a 475-ml/16-fl oz measure of basmati rice

450 g/1 lb tomatoes, coarsely chopped

about 250 ml/8 fl oz chicken stock, if needed

2 tablespoons olive or rapeseed oil

10 peppercorns

5 cloves

1 x 5–7.5-cm/2–3-inch cinnamon stick

2 bay leaves

1 medium onion, peeled and cut into fine half-rings

1½ teaspoons salt

Put the rice in a bowl. Cover with cold water, and stir the rice gently. Pour out the dirty water. Do this 4 or 5 times. Now cover well with fresh water and leave to soak for 30 minutes (longer will not hurt). Drain and leave in a sieve set over a bowl to drain further.

Put the tomatoes in a blender and liquidise completely. Strain and pour into a measuring jug. Add enough chicken stock or water to make 650 ml/22 fl oz.

Preheat the oven to 160°C/gas mark 3.

Pour the oil into a heavy-based ovenproof pan with a lid and set over a medium–high heat. When hot, put in the peppercorns, cloves, cinnamon and bay leaves. Stir a few times, then put in the onion. Stir and fry until it turns a reddish colour. Add the drained rice. Stir very gently, scraping the bottom, for 1 minute. Now add the tomato liquid and salt. Stir and bring to the boil. Cover the pan tightly with foil, crimping the edges, and then with the lid. Place in the oven and bake for 30 minutes.

Basmati Rice with Lentils

We eat this very nutritious rice dish a lot and frequently serve it to our guests. It is almost a meal in itself, and may be served simply with Yoghurt Sauce (see page 188) and any vegetable you like

Serves 6

a 120-ml/4-fl oz measure of brown or green lentils

a 475-ml/16-fl oz measure of basmati rice

3 tablespoons olive or rapeseed oil

2 x 5-cm/2-inch cinnamon sticks

8 cardamom pods

2 bay leaves

½ medium onion, peeled and cut into fine half-rings

1½ teaspoons salt

Soak the lentils in warm water for 3–5 hours. Drain.

Put the rice in a bowl. Cover with cold water, and stir the rice gently. Pour out the dirty water. Do this 4 or 5 times. Now cover well with fresh water and leave to soak for 30 minutes (longer will not hurt). Drain and leave in a sieve set over a bowl to drain further.

Pour the oil into a heavy-based medium pan that has a tight-fitting lid and set over a medium–high heat. When hot, put in the cinnamon, cardamom and bay leaves. Stir for 10 seconds. Put in the onion. Stir and fry until it turns reddish-brown. Add the lentils, rice and salt. Reduce the heat to medium and sauté the rice very gently for 1 minute. Add 700 ml/24 fl oz water and bring to the boil. Cover tightly, reduce the heat to very, very low and cook gently for 25 minutes.

Rice with Moong Dal (*Dry Khichri*)

One of the oldest Indian dishes and continuously popular these thousands of years is khichri, a dish of rice and split peas. Starting around the Raj period, the British began to serve a version of khichri for breakfast in their country homes: they removed the dal and added fish, and called it 'kedgeree'. There are two main versions of the original dish: one is dry, like well-cooked rice, where each grain is separate, and the other is wet, like a porridge. Both are delicious. The first is more elegant, the second more soothing. Below is the first, dry version. Serve it like rice, with all manner of curries **Serves 6**

a 350-ml/12-fl oz measure of basmati rice

a 120-ml/4-fl oz measure of skinned and split moong dal

3 tablespoons olive or rapeseed oil

½ teaspoon whole cumin seeds

1 small onion, peeled and cut into fine half-rings

1 teaspoon salt

Combine the rice and moong dal. Wash gently in several changes of water. Drain. Cover generously with fresh water and leave to soak for 2 hours. Drain well.

Pour the oil into a heavy-based medium pan and set over a medium–high heat. When hot, put in the cumin seeds and a few seconds later the onion. Stir and fry until the onion has turned reddish-brown. Now add the drained rice and dal. Stir very gently for 1 minute. Add the salt and 650 ml/22 fl oz water. Bring to the boil. Cover tightly, reduce the heat to very, very low and cook gently for 25 minutes.

Prawn Biryani
A refreshing rice dish that may be served with vegetables, bean and split-pea dishes, and chutneys. Sometimes I eat it all by itself with a large green salad **Serves 4–6**

a 450-ml/15-fl oz measure of basmati rice

450 g/1 lb medium-sized raw, headless prawns, peeled and deveined (340 g/12 oz prepared weight)

3 cloves garlic, peeled and crushed

1 teaspoon ground cumin

½ teaspoon ground turmeric

¼ teaspoon cayenne pepper, or to taste

freshly ground black pepper

salt

3 tablespoons olive or rapeseed oil

4 teaspoons lemon juice

4 tablespoons chopped fresh coriander or parsley

4 cardamom pods

600 ml/20 fl oz chicken stock

Put the rice in a bowl. Cover with cold water, and stir gently. Pour out the dirty water. Do this 4 or 5 times. Now cover well with fresh water and leave to soak for 30 minutes (longer will not hurt). Drain and leave in a sieve set over a bowl to drain further.

Halve the prawns crossways. Sprinkle the garlic, cumin, turmeric, cayenne pepper, black pepper and ⅓ teaspoon salt over the prawns, rubbing them in. Cover and set aside.

Pour the oil into a heavy-based medium pan and set over a medium–high heat. When hot, put in the prawns and stir for 2–3 minutes, or until they become opaque. Remove with a slotted spoon and put in a bowl. Add the lemon juice and fresh coriander. Stir and taste for balance of seasonings.

Put the cardamom and stock into the pan used for the prawns and bring to the boil, scraping the bottom to release the seasonings. Add the drained rice, ½ teaspoon salt if the stock is salted and 1 teaspoon if it is not, and bring to the boil. Cover tightly, reduce the heat to very low and cook for 25 minutes.

Put the prawns and their juices over the top of the rice, cover quickly and keep cooking for another minute. Turn off the heat. Stir gently and keep covered until needed.

Plain Jasmine Rice

Jasmine rice is very different in texture and taste from basmati rice. It is more clingy, more spongy and more glutinous, and, at its best, has a jasmine-like aroma. One some days it is exactly the soothing rice I yearn for. It is certainly closer to the daily rice eaten in south, east and west India, where basmati rice is reserved for special occasions only. Look for good-quality jasmine rice, usually sold by Thai and other oriental grocers. Sadly, price is often a good indication. I do not usually bother to wash it **Serves 6**

a 475-ml/16-fl oz measure of jasmine rice

Put the rice in a heavy-based pan along with 700 ml/24 fl oz water. Bring to a rolling boil. Cover tightly, reduce the heat to very, very low and cook gently for 25 minutes.

Coconut Rice

This is such a soothing rice dish – slightly sweet and salty, with just a hint of black pepper. (Do not eat the peppercorns – they are just for flavouring. Push them to the side of your plate.) As the dish is south Indian, I have made it with jasmine rice, which is closer in texture to the shorter-grained rices commonly found in that region. I love to serve this with northern lamb and chicken curries, thus breaking tradition and combining north and south in an exciting new way   **Serves 6**

3 tablespoons olive or rapeseed oil

½ teaspoon whole peppercorns

70 g/2½ oz peeled and finely sliced shallots

a 475-ml/16-fl oz measure of jasmine rice

1½ teaspoons salt

½ teaspoon ground turmeric

350 ml/12 fl oz coconut milk, from a well-shaken can, mixed with an equal measure of water

Preheat the oven to 160°C/gas mark 3.

Pour the oil into a heavy-based ovenproof pan with a lid and set over a medium–high heat. When hot, put in the peppercorns. Let them sizzle for a few seconds. Add the shallots and stir-fry until they turn reddish-brown. Add the rice, salt and turmeric. Reduce the heat to low and stir gently for 1 minute.

Add the coconut milk mixture, increase the heat to medium–high and bring to a rolling boil. Cover the pan with foil, crimping the edges, and then with the lid. Place in the oven for 30 minutes. Remove from the oven. Quickly fluff up the rice with a fork, then cover again and leave to rest for 15 minutes.

Yoghurt Rice

Yoghurt Rice There are hundreds of versions of this salad-like dish, which are eaten throughout south India and parts of western India as well. At its base is rice, the local starch and staple. The rice is cooked until it is quite soft. Then yoghurt, and sometimes a little milk as well, is added, as well as any fruit, raw vegetables or lightly blanched vegetables that one likes. The final step is what makes the salad completely Indian. A tiny amount of oil is heated and spices, such as mustard seeds, curry leaves and red chillies, are thrown into it. This mixture is poured over the rice to give it pungency and its reason for being. It is best served at room temperature, without being refrigerated. Other salads may be added to the meal. It can also be used as a topping for soups **Serves 4 as a salad**

a 250-ml/8-fl oz measure of jasmine rice

1¼ teaspoons salt

4 tablespoons cold milk

120 ml/4 fl oz natural yoghurt, preferably Greek or 'bio', lightly beaten with a fork or whisk

3–4 cherry tomatoes, quartered and lightly salted

4 tablespoons finely chopped fresh coriander

2 teaspoons olive or rapeseed oil

¼ teaspoon skinned urad dal or yellow split peas or lightly crushed raw peanuts

½ teaspoon whole brown mustard seeds

2–3 whole dried, hot red chillies

10–12 fresh curry leaves (optional), torn

Combine the rice, 700 ml/24 fl oz water and the salt in a medium pan and bring to the boil. Cover tightly, reduce the heat to very, very low and cook for 25 minutes. Empty the rice into a wide bowl and add the milk. Stir to mix and cool off the rice a bit. Now add the yoghurt and mix again. Add the tomatoes and coriander. Mix again.

Pour the oil into a small pan or frying pan and set over a medium–high heat. When hot, put in the urad dal. Let it turn reddish. Put in the mustard seeds and chillies. As soon as the seeds pop and the chillies darken, add the curry leaves. A second later, pour the oil and spices over the rice mixture. Stir to mix.

Plain Brown Rice

South Asians do not really eat brown rice, but much of south India, western coastal India and Sri Lanka eat a very nutritious red rice. The grains have a red hull that is only partially milled. This is eaten plain and also ground into flours to make pancakes and noodles. This recipe works for all the brown rices available in the West. This may be served with all South Asian meals **Serves 3–4**

a 250-ml/8-fl oz measure of brown rice

½ teaspoon salt (optional)

Put the rice, 475 ml/16 fl oz water and salt (if using) in a small, heavy-based pan with a tight-fitting lid. Bring to the boil. Cover tightly, reduce the heat to very, very low and cook for 45 minutes.

Take the covered pan off the heat and leave for 10 minutes before serving.

Curried Brown Rice

Here is a recipe I have devised for the brown rices (and mixtures that combine brown rice with wild rice) usually found in Western markets. Served with vegetables and a yoghurt relish, this dish makes a fine vegetarian meal. You may also serve this with meat and fish curries **Serves 3–4**

2 tablespoons olive or rapeseed oil

4 cardamom pods

1 x 5-cm/2-inch cinnamon stick

5 tablespoons peeled and chopped onions

⅛ teaspoon ground turmeric

½ teaspoon ground cumin

⅛ teaspoon cayenne pepper

a 250-ml/8-fl oz measure of brown rice

475 ml/16 fl oz chicken or vegetable stock

salt

Pour the oil into a small, heavy-based pan and set over a medium–high heat. When hot, put in the cardamom and cinnamon. Stir once or twice, then add the onions. Stir and fry until they brown at the edges. Lower the heat to medium and put in the turmeric, cumin and cayenne pepper. Stir once and put in the rice, stock and ¼ teaspoon salt if the stock is salted, ½ teaspoon if it is not. Stir and bring to the boil. Cover tightly, reduce the heat to very low and cook for 45 minutes.

Take the covered pan off the heat and leave for 10 minutes before serving.

Semolina Pilaf with Peas

Here is one of the great offerings from Kerala, a state on the south-west coast of India, where it is known as *uppama*. The semolina that is required here is a coarse-grained variety that is sold as *sooji* or *rava* in Indian shops. (It is not the very fine version used to make pasta, nor the type used for semolina pudding.) This pilaf-like dish may be eaten for breakfast with milky coffee and an accompanying coconut chutney (see Sri Lankan Cooked Coconut Chutney, page 241), or as a snack with tea, or as part of a meal as the exquisite starch **Serves 3–4**

140 g/5 oz peas, defrosted if frozen

salt

2 tablespoons olive or rapeseed oil

⅛ teaspoon ground asafoetida

½ teaspoon skinned urad dal or yellow split peas

½ teaspoon whole brown mustard seeds

10 fresh curry leaves or 5 fresh basil leaves, torn

½ teaspoon peeled and very finely grated fresh ginger

2–4 fresh, hot green chillies (such as bird's eye), finely chopped

180 g/6 oz coarse semolina (see above)

2 tablespoons finely chopped fresh coriander

2 teaspoons lemon juice

1 teaspoon caster sugar

Boil the peas with a little salt long enough to just cook them, then drain.

Put 475 ml/16 fl oz water in a small pan and bring to the boil. Reduce the heat to very low and leave.

Pour the oil into a non-stick frying pan and set over a medium–high heat. When hot, put in the asafoetida and urad dal. Wait 2 seconds and put in the mustard seeds. As soon as the dal turns red and the mustard seeds pop, a matter of seconds, put in the curry leaves, ginger and chillies. Stir for a few seconds, then add the semolina and 1 teaspoon salt. Stir and cook for 3–4 minutes or until the semolina is very lightly browned.

Lower the heat. Now begin to add the boiling water from the small pan a few tablespoons at a time over the next 7 minutes, stirring and breaking up the lumps as you do so. Add the peas and coriander. Keep cooking and stirring over a very low heat another 3–4 minutes, or until all the grains puff up. Add the lemon juice and sugar and stir to mix.

Bulgar Pilaf with Peas & Tomato

Bulgar, a wheat that has been cooked, cracked and dried, is used in parts of the Punjab (north-western India) to make a variety of nutritious pilafs. Generally, two grades of bulgar are sold by Indian and Middle Eastern grocers: coarse-grained and fine-grained. The coarser-grained bulgar is ideal here. Serve as you would a rice pilaf (see Rice Pilaf with Almonds & Sultanas page 203) **Serves 4**

3 tablespoons olive or rapeseed oil

½ teaspoon whole cumin seeds

1 teaspoon peeled and very finely grated fresh ginger

1 medium tomato, very finely chopped

140 g/5 oz peas, defrosted if frozen

a 250-ml/8-fl oz measure of coarse bulgar wheat

¼ teaspoon cayenne pepper

¾ teaspoon salt

Pour the oil into a smallish, heavy-based pan with a tight-fitting lid over a medium–high heat. When hot, put in the cumin seeds. Ten seconds later put in the ginger. Stir once and add the tomato. Stir for 1 minute, then add the peas, bulgar, cayenne pepper and salt. Lower the heat to medium and stir gently for 1 minute. Add 350 ml/12 fl oz water and bring to a simmer. Cover tightly, reduce the heat to very, very low and cook gently for 35 minutes.

Turn off the heat. Lift the lid and quickly put a tea towel over the pilaf. Cover again with the lid and leave in a warm place for 20 minutes, allowing the towel to absorb some of the moisture. Fluff up with a fork and serve.

Thin Rice Noodles (*Idiappam*)

Throughout southern India and Sri Lanka fine, home-made, steamed rice noodles are often served at mealtimes instead of rice and are known as *idiappam* (or string hoppers) in India, and *idiappa* in Sri Lanka. Since making them is somewhat cumbersome, requiring a special mould and steaming equipment, I do the next best thing. I buy dried rice sticks from Thai grocers and reconstitute them. These noodles could be served at breakfast with a little sugar and cardamom-flavoured coconut milk, and at major meals with curries – though I have to say that, to my great delight, I have had them with fish curries for breakfast in Sri Lanka, and with fiery fish curries for dinner in Kerala **Serves 4**

180 g/6 oz dried rice sticks

Soak the rice sticks in a large bowl of cold water that covers them completely for 2–3 hours. Shortly before eating, drain them and put them back in the bowl. With a pair of kitchen scissors, snip the noodles into manageable lengths. Pour boiling water over them. Leave for 1 minute, then drain and serve.

Thin Rice Noodles with Brussels Sprouts
This south Indian-style dish may also be made with shredded cabbage. You will notice that a little raw rice is used here as a seasoning. It provides a nutty texture. Serve with a lamb or beef curry or grilled meats **Serves 4**

180 g/6 oz dried rice sticks (from Thai grocers)

225 g/8 oz Brussels sprouts

2 tablespoons olive or rapeseed oil

½ teaspoon any raw white rice

½ teaspoon whole brown mustard seeds

4 whole hot, dried red chillies

10–15 fresh curry leaves or 5 fresh basil leaves, torn

1 teaspoon salt

Soak the rice sticks in a large bowl of cold water that covers them completely for 2–3 hours. Drain and leave in the strainer. With a pair of kitchen scissors, snip the noodles into manageable lengths.

Trim the sprouts. Cut each in half lengthways, then cut crossways into shreds 5 mm/¼ inch thick.

Pour the oil into a non-stick frying pan and set over a medium–high heat. When hot, put in the rice. Five seconds later, add the mustard seeds and chillies. As soon as the seeds start to pop, a matter of seconds, put in the curry leaves and the sprouts. Stir and fry for 5 minutes, or until the sprouts are lightly browned. Add 120 ml/4 fl oz water and cover. Lower the heat and cook for 1 minute.

Add the prepared rice noodles and salt. Stir for 3–4 minutes. Add 250 ml/8 fl oz water and bring to a simmer. Cover and cook over a very low heat for 5 minutes, stirring frequently.

Chapati (Wholemeal Flatbread)

A chapati is like a tortilla, but unlike both the corn and the wheat tortilla, it is made out of wholemeal flour, known as *ata* or *chapati* flour. Instead of rolling each one out with a rolling pin, you may use a tortilla press or a chapati press. Small, thin chapatis (about 13 cm/5 inches in diameter) are considered much more elegant than large, thick ones, such as the ones shown opposite, though you will find all sizes in the cities and villages of India. Those who eat chapatis daily eat them with everything at lunch and dinner. You break off a piece and enfold meat or vegetable in it. You could also roll up some food inside a whole chapati to make a 'wrap', though you would not do this at the table, only with leftovers to make a snack **Makes 6**

130 g/4½ oz chapati flour or an equal mixture of sifted wholemeal and plain flour, plus extra for dusting

butter or ghee (optional)

Make a soft dough using all the flour and about 120 ml/4 fl oz water. Knead well for 10 minutes. Roll into a ball and either put it in a plastic bag or a bowl covered with a damp cloth. Leave for at least 15–30 minutes, or refrigerate it for up to 2 days for future use.

Set a cast-iron frying pan or crêpe pan over a medium–high heat and allow to heat up.

Knead the dough again, then divide it into 6 balls. Keep 5 covered. Flour your work surface and roll the ball out evenly into a 13.5-cm/5¼-inch circle. Pick the chapati up and slap it around between your two palms to remove some of the flour. Now slap it into the hot pan. Cook for 10 seconds. Flip it over. Cook the second side for 10 seconds. Flip it over again and cook for 10 seconds. Flip it a third time and do the same. Now pick up the chapati and put it in your microwave oven. Blast it for about 30 seconds on full power, or until puffed. (If you have no microwave, press down on different parts of the chapati with a small wad of cloth as you give it a slight turn in the pan.) Remove, brush with butter or ghee, if desired, and keep covered.

Using a piece of slightly damp kitchen paper, wipe out the pan. Reduce the heat to medium–low while you roll out your second chapati and proceed as before, turning the heat up again before you slap the next chapati on to the hot surface.

Poori

Poori (Deep-fried Puffed Bread) A poori (pictured overleaf) requires the same dough as the chapati, except there is a little oil in it. It is rolled out in almost the same way, but then, instead of being cooked on a hot, griddle-like surface, it is quickly deep-fried in hot oil, making it puff up like a balloon. Pooris may be eaten with all curries and vegetables. At breakfast they are often served with potato dishes, such as Potato & Pea Curry or Potatoes with Cumin & Mustard Seeds (see pages 167 and 168), and hot pickles and chutneys. We always took pooris on picnics, stacked up tightly inside a tin. Of course they became quite flat, but still tasted wonderful. On picnics they were eaten with minced meat dishes and pickles, all at room temperature **Makes 12**

260 g/9 oz chapati flour or an equal mixture of sifted wholemeal and plain flour

½ teaspoon salt

olive or rapeseed oil, for the dough and deep-frying

about 250 ml/8 fl oz milk or water

Put the flour and salt into a bowl. Dribble in 1 tablespoon oil and rub it into the flour. Slowly add enough milk or water so that you can gather all the dough together into a ball. Knead for 10 minutes until smooth. Roll into a ball. Rub the ball with a little oil and slip it into a plastic bag. Seal and leave for 30 minutes.

Pour some oil for deep-frying into a *karhai*, wok or frying pan and set over a medium heat. In a wok the oil should extend over a diameter of at least 15 cm/6 inches. In a frying pan you will need at least a 2.5-cm/1-inch depth of oil. Allow it time to heat up. Keep a large baking sheet lined with kitchen paper next to you. While the oil is heating, knead the dough again and divide it into 12 balls. Keep them covered. Take one ball and rub it lightly with oil. Now flatten it into a patty and roll it out into a 13–14-cm/5–5½-inch circle. Lift it up and lay it on top of the hot oil without allowing it to fold up. It may well sink, but should rise to the surface almost immediately. Now, using the back of a slotted spoon, keep pushing the poori under the surface of the oil with rapid, light strokes. It will resist and puff up in seconds. Turn it over and count up to 2. Now lift the poori out of the oil and deposit it on the paper-lined baking sheet.

Make all the pooris in this way. Stack and cover tightly in foil if not eating right away.

Paratha (Griddle Bread)

The dough for parathas is similar to that for pooris, but is rolled out very differently to give it multiple layers. It is cooked on a cast-iron griddle, rather like a pancake, with butter, ghee or oil to keep it lubricated. This particular paratha is triangular in shape. Parathas are a very popular breakfast food when they are eaten with yoghurt and pickles. They may also be served at mealtimes with meats and vegetables **Makes 8**

190 g/6¾ oz chapati flour or an equal mixture of sifted wholemeal and plain flour

½ teaspoon salt

1 tablespoon olive or rapeseed oil, plus a little extra for rubbing the dough

about 4 tablespoons melted butter or ghee

Put the flour and salt into a bowl. Dribble in the oil and rub it in with your fingertips. Slowly add about 120 ml/4 fl oz or more water and gather all the flour together. You are aiming for a soft dough. Knead for 8–10 minutes. Form into a ball. Rub it with oil and slip it into a plastic bag for 30 minutes.

Set a cast-iron frying pan, griddle or crêpe pan over a medium heat.

Meanwhile, knead the dough again and divide it into 8 equal-sized balls. Keep them covered. Take 1 ball and flatten it a bit, then, on a floured surface, roll it out into a 13-cm/5-inch circle. Brush the surface with butter and fold in half. Brush the top with more butter and fold in half again, forming a triangle. Roll out the triangle on a floured surface, keeping its basic shape, until the three sides are each about 13 cm/5 inches long.

Brush the griddle with butter and slap the paratha on to it. As soon as one side is golden (a few dark spots are fine), turn it over and add a little more butter. Adjust the heat if necessary. Do not let the paratha become brittle. Remove and wrap in foil. Make all the parathas in this way.

The foil bundle may be reheated in a medium oven (180°C/ gas mark 4), or individual parathas may be heated for about 30 seconds each on full power in a microwave oven.

Relishes & Accompaniments

South Asians demand a lot of their meals: they want them to be soothing, comforting and nourishing; they insist upon contrasting flavours and textures; they also demand that every mouthful be full of titillating, varying possibilities.

The last is achieved with the relishes that are served with every single meal. 'Relish' is a wide, loose term. Think of the pickles served at a Jewish, New York delicatessen, or the mustard and horseradish served with English roast beef, or the *rouille* served with a French fish soup. They all add 'a little something', a little pep. South Asians often have more than one such item at the table. The reasons are partly nutritional – yoghurt relishes add protein, fresh chutneys made from herbs or tamarind add vitamins and iron, and fresh salads add roughage.

But there is more to it than that. This part of the world likes each mouthful to have the possibilities of variation. Individuals might decide not to exercise that option, but they want it available to them. Hence all the relishes at the table.

Not all relishes are made the day they are eaten. The pickles might have been made months earlier, or even be shop-bought; the sweet, preserve-type chutneys might be sitting in the store-cupboard, or might also have been bought; all that needs to be prepared on the same day is the yoghurt relish, the fresh green or red chutney and the salad, which could be as basic as sliced raw onions with tomatoes and cucumbers.

Even if you are poor and eating a very simple meal of rice/bread and beans, you can add a little yoghurt to one mouthful, a little pickle to the next, a bit of salad – to the third, and some fresh chutney to the fourth. The world is your oyster. You are now a king or queen in your own home!

Salaad

My north Indian family called this *salaad* (salad), but similar salads with varying seasonings are known in some parts of India as *cachumbar*. These salads generally contain onions (our Indian red onions), cucumbers and tomatoes but, according to the seasons, we in Delhi could find radishes or kohlrabi in them as well. In some parts of India barely sprouted mung beans and peanuts could be added. This fresh salad was always at our table in some form at every meal, with the simplest of dressings added at the last minute. There was never any oil in the dressing. Instead, there was fresh lime juice, salt, pepper, chilli powder and roasted ground cumin seeds. We just put a generous dollop on our plates (or side plates) and ate it with everything   **Serves 4**

140 g/5 oz peeled cucumbers, cut into 7-mm/⅓-inch dice

7 large cherry tomatoes, quartered, or 12 smaller tomatoes, halved

1 large shallot, peeled and cut into fine slivers

½ teaspoon salt

freshly ground black pepper

½ teaspoon ground roasted cumin seeds (see page 263)

⅛ teaspoon cayenne pepper

1 tablespoon lime or lemon juice

Combine the cucumbers, tomatoes and shallot in a bowl. Just before serving, add the remaining ingredients. Toss to mix.

Cucumber Salad, North Indian-style

In much of India a fresh salad is present at every single meal. This kind of cucumber salad was something that my mother threw together moments before we sat down to eat. Ideally, cucumbers with tiny undeveloped seeds should be used because they have the best texture, but when cucumbers are growing wildly in my garden, and some that have hidden themselves amongst the leaves have grown beyond the best picking size, I pick them anyway, peel them and scoop out their seeds. They still make good eating. **Serves 4–6**

425 g/15 oz peeled and sliced cucumber (about 1½ whole cucumbers)

¾ teaspoon salt

freshly ground black pepper

¼ teaspoon cayenne pepper or finely crushed red pepper

1–2 teaspoons lemon juice

8–10 fresh mint leaves, chopped

Peel the cucumbers and cut in half lengthways (this is not necessary if the cucumbers are very slim). Cut crossways into thin slices or chunks, as desired. Put in a bowl and add all the remaining ingredients. Toss to mix. Taste and adjust the seasonings as needed.

Okra Sambol

This Sri Lankan *sambol* may best be described as an accompanying salad or relish to be served at curry meals. You can make it as hot as you like   **Serves 3**

3 tablespoons olive or rapeseed oil

225 g/8 oz okra, topped and tailed, and cut crossways into 1-cm/½-inch pieces

45 g/1½ oz red onion, peeled and cut into very fine half-rings (if the onion is large, cut into quarter-rings)

½–¾ teaspoon salt

⅛–¼ teaspoon cayenne pepper

freshly ground black pepper

2–3 teaspoons lemon juice

Pour the oil into a frying pan and set over a medium–high heat. When hot, put in the okra. Stir and fry for 6–7 minutes, or until the okra is lightly browned. Remove with a slotted spoon and put in a bowl.

Add all the remaining ingredients to the bowl. Mix well and taste, adjusting the flavours to get the perfect balance.

Cauliflower Cachumbar

This is a salad from India's western state of Gujarat. If you like nuts, two tablespoons of crushed roasted peanuts could be stirred in just before serving. It may be served with most Indian meals and lasts several days in the refrigerator if kept covered **Serves 4**

250 g/9 oz cauliflower, chopped into pieces no larger than 7 x 5 mm/⅓ x ¼ inch)

1 teaspoon salt

½ teaspoon cayenne pepper

1 teaspoon finely chopped hot, green chilli (such as bird's eye, green cayenne or jalapeño)

3–4 tablespoons chopped fresh coriander

½ teaspoon caster sugar

2 tablespoons lemon juice

2 teaspoons red or white wine vinegar

1 tablespoon olive or rapeseed oil

½ teaspoon whole brown or yellow mustard seeds

Put the cauliflower in a bowl. Add the salt and rub it in, mixing well. Set aside for 1–3 hours in the refrigerator.

If any liquid has accumulated with the cauliflower, drain it off. Add the cayenne pepper, chilli, coriander, sugar, lemon juice and vinegar. Mix well.

Pour the oil into a small pan and set over a medium–high heat. When hot, put in the mustard seeds. As soon as they begin to pop, a matter of seconds, pour the contents of the pan over the cauliflower. Stir to mix.

Thin Raw Onion Rings

Indians love raw onion rings with their kebabs, just as many people like a slice of onion with their hamburgers. Browned meat and raw onions; it is a marriage made in heaven. The Indian rings are different, though. They are made from smaller onions and are cut paper-thin. To moderate the sharpness, they are soaked in cold water and dried off thoroughly in a clean tea towel. The rings separate into a tangled mound

Serves 4–6

2 medium onions, peeled

Cut the onions crosswise into the finest rings possible. Soak them in a bowl of icy water for 30 minutes. Drain well and dry thoroughly in a clean tea towel, twisting the towel if needed. Place in a bowl and serve.

Vinegar-Chilli-Onion Dipping Sauce

This simple sauce is perfect for spooning over fried fish or chicken, grilled meats and any kind of kebab **Serves 2–3**

2 tablespoons red wine vinegar (or any vinegar you like)

1 tablespoon peeled and very finely sliced shallot or onion, cut into fine quarter-rings

⅛ teaspoon cayenne pepper

⅛–¼ teaspoon salt

6–8 fresh mint leaves, finely chopped (optional)

Mix all the ingredients together in a small bowl and leave for 30 minutes to steep.

Fresh Green Chutney

A fresh chutney to serve with all Indian meals, this has a shelf life of two to three days if stored in the refrigerator. What is not used up may be frozen for another day   **Serves 8**

4 teaspoons lime or lemon juice

1 smallish (85-g/3-oz) tomato, chopped

¾ teaspoon salt

3 fresh, hot green chillies (such as bird's eye), chopped

30 g/1 oz chopped fresh coriander

20 fresh mint leaves

60 g/2 oz grated fresh coconut, defrosted if frozen

Put 3 tablespoons water, the lime juice, tomato, salt and chillies into a blender. Blend thoroughly. Add the coriander and mint. Blend again until smooth.

Finally, add the coconut and blend some more, pushing down with a rubber spatula if necessary, until the chutney is smooth.

Peshawari Red Pepper Chutney

This hot, savoury chutney is from what used to be India's north-west frontier, but is now on Pakistan's border with Afghanistan. There it is made with fresh red chillies, which have a beautiful colour and medium heat. They are not always easy to find, so I use a mixture of red peppers and cayenne pepper. They are always combined with nuts, generally almonds, but sometimes walnuts. This chutney may be frozen. It is like gold in the bank. Serve it with kebabs, fritters and with a general meal

Serves 8

½ large red pepper, seeded and coarsely chopped

20 large or 30 small fresh mint leaves, coarsely chopped

2 tablespoons lemon juice

1 clove garlic, peeled and coarsely chopped

½ teaspoon cayenne pepper

½ teaspoon salt

freshly ground black pepper

1 tablespoon slivered, blanched almonds or chopped walnuts

1 teaspoon chopped fresh dill

Put the red pepper, mint, lemon juice, garlic, cayenne pepper, salt and black pepper into a blender in the order listed and blend until smooth. Add the almonds and blend again. Pour into a bowl and check for seasonings. Mix in the dill.

Bengali-style Tomato Chutney

At Bengali banquets this chutney, along with deep-fried, puffed white flour breads (loochis) and poppadoms, is served as the penultimate course, just before the dessert. In the Western world I tend to serve it with the main meal: I layer it thickly on to hamburgers, serve dollops with fried/roast chicken and roast lamb, use it as a spread for cheese sandwiches, and, at Indian meals, offer it as a relish with my kebabs and curries **Makes a generous 350 ml/12 fl oz**

2 tablespoons olive, rapeseed or peanut oil

½ teaspoon whole cumin seeds

½ teaspoon whole brown or yellow mustard seeds

¼ teaspoon whole fennel seeds

475 ml/16 fl oz tomato passata (see page 268)

1½ teaspoons peeled and very finely grated fresh ginger

175 ml/6 fl oz cider vinegar

200 g/7 oz caster sugar

¾ teaspoon red pepper flakes

1¼ teaspoons salt

2 tablespoons sultanas (optional)

Pour the oil into a heavy-based, medium stainless-steel pan and set over a medium–high heat. When hot, put in the cumin and mustard seeds. As soon as the mustard seeds begin to pop, a matter of seconds, add the fennel seeds. A few seconds later, put in the tomato passata, ginger, vinegar, sugar, pepper flakes and salt. Stir and bring to a simmer. Once bubbling, lower the heat and simmer, uncovered, stirring now and then, for about 50 minutes. Add the sultanas and cook for another 10 minutes. The finished chutney should be thick and have a glazed appearance.

Spoon into a sterilised jar. Allow to cool, then screw the lid on and refrigerate. It will keep for several months.

Peanut Chutney with Sesame Seeds

Although this may be served with all Indian meals, it is particularly good with grilled meats and kebabs, and makes an exciting dip for vegetables and all manner of crisps and fritters. You could also use it instead of butter in a sandwich: try it with cheese, turkey, tomato and lettuce **Makes about 7–8 tablespoons**

2 tablespoons peanut butter, preferably unsalted

2 tablespoons natural yoghurt

1 tablespoon lemon juice

1 tablespoon peeled and finely chopped shallot

1 tablespoon finely chopped fresh coriander

½–¾ teaspoon cayenne pepper

¼ teaspoon salt

1 teaspoon olive or rapeseed oil

1 teaspoon whole sesame seeds

Put the peanut butter in a small bowl with 1 tablespoon water, the yoghurt, lemon juice, shallot, coriander, cayenne pepper and salt (if using salted peanut butter, taste before adding any more salt). Mix until smooth. Taste for balance of seasonings.

Pour the oil into a small, heavy-based frying pan and set over a medium heat. When hot, put in the sesame seeds. Shake until they either brown slightly or begin to pop. Add both seeds and oil to the chutney. Stir to mix.

Sri Lankan Cooked Coconut Chutney

This delightful chutney is served with all manner of savoury steamed rice cakes and pancakes. I love it with the Semolina Pilaf on page 216, but it may be served with most Indian meals. It will keep in the refrigerator for two to three days, and leftovers may be frozen **Serves 6–8**

1 tablespoon lime or lemon juice

2 cloves garlic, peeled and chopped

½ teaspoon salt

3 fresh, hot green chillies (such as bird's eye), chopped

¼ teaspoon whole cumin seeds

1 medium shallot, peeled, one half chopped, the other half cut into fine slivers

20–25 fresh curry leaves, if available

60 g/2 oz grated fresh coconut, defrosted if frozen

1 tablespoon olive or rapeseed oil

¼ teaspoon whole brown mustard seeds

Put 120 ml/4 fl oz water, the lime juice, the garlic, salt, chillies, cumin, chopped shallot and 10–15 curry leaves into a blender in the order listed and blend thoroughly. Add the coconut and blend thoroughly again.

Pour the oil into a small pan and set over a medium heat. When hot, put in the mustard seeds. As soon as they pop, a matter of seconds, add the 10 remaining curry leaves and the sliced shallot. Stir and cook until the shallot softens slightly, then add the contents of the blender. Stir and bring to a simmer. Simmer very gently for 1 minute, then turn off the heat. Serve warm or at room temperature.

Sri Lankan Coconut Sambol

This is Sri Lanka's everyday coconut sambol. Known as *pol sambol*, it would be called a chutney in India. It may be served with any meal   **Serves 6**

1 tablespoon lime or lemon juice

½ teaspoon salt

1½ teaspoons cayenne pepper

1 teaspoon sweet red paprika

60 g/2 oz grated fresh coconut, defrosted if frozen

Put 150 ml/5 fl oz water into a blender. Add all the ingredients in the order listed and blend until you have a smooth paste.

Yoghurt Sambol with Tomato & Shallot

This yoghurt relish comes from the Tamil communities of Sri Lanka, where it is called 'curd sambol'. It may be served with most South Asian meals, and also eaten at lunch, like a salad   **Serves 4**

250 ml/8 fl oz natural yoghurt

¼–½ teaspoon salt

freshly ground black pepper

⅛–¼ teaspoon cayenne pepper

1 medium tomato, cut into small dice

1 medium shallot, peeled and chopped finely

1 tablespoon olive or rapeseed oil

¼ teaspoon whole brown mustard seeds

8–10 fresh curry leaves or 4 fresh basil leaves, torn

Put the yoghurt in a bowl. Mix gently with a whisk or fork until smooth and creamy. Add the salt, pepper, cayenne pepper, tomato and shallot. Mix.

Pour the oil into a very small pan and set over a medium–high heat. When hot, put in the mustard seeds. As soon as they start to pop, a matter of seconds, add the curry leaves, then quickly empty the contents of the pan into the bowl of yoghurt. Stir to mix.

Yoghurt with Pineapple

Somewhere between a relish and a curry, this may be served with most Indian meals **Serves 4**

300 g/11 oz fresh pineapple, cut into 1-cm/½-inch cubes

2 tablespoons caster sugar

3 tablespoons finely grated coconut (frozen or desiccated may be used, see page 263)

250 ml/8 fl oz natural yoghurt

1¼–1½ teaspoons salt

1 fresh green chilli (such as bird's eye), finely chopped

1 tablespoon olive or rapeseed oil

½ teaspoon whole brown mustard seeds

¼ teaspoon whole cumin seeds

2 hot, dried red chillies

10 fresh curry leaves or 6 fresh basil leaves, torn

2 tablespoons peeled and finely sliced shallot or onion, cut into fine half-rings

Combine the pineapple, sugar and 120 ml/4 fl oz water in a pan. Bring to a simmer. Stir and cook over a low heat until the liquid evaporates, about 10 minutes. Add the coconut and stir once or twice. Take off the heat and set aside to cool.

Put the yoghurt in a bowl and beat lightly with a fork or whisk until smooth and creamy. Add the salt, green chilli and cooled pineapple mixture. Stir to mix.

Pour the oil into a small frying pan and set over a medium–high heat. When hot, put in the mustard seeds, cumin seeds and red chillies. As soon as the mustard seeds start to pop, a matter of seconds, put in the curry leaves and shallot. Reduce the heat to medium. Stir and cook until the shallot starts to brown. Now pour the contents of the frying pan into the bowl of pineapple yoghurt and stir it in.

Sweet-sour Yoghurt with Apple & Shallot

Yoghurt relishes are eaten with meals throughout India. They are nearly always savoury, though in Western states, such as Gujarat, a little sugar is added as well as the salt to give a sweet-sour-salty flavour **Serves 4–6**

300 ml/10 fl oz natural
  yoghurt

¼–½ teaspoon salt

freshly ground black pepper

⅛–¼ teaspoon cayenne pepper

1 teaspoon caster sugar

¼ teaspoon peeled and finely
  grated fresh ginger

½ Granny Smith apple, peeled,
  cored and coarsely grated

2 tablespoons olive or
  rapeseed oil

¼ teaspoon whole cumin seeds

1 small shallot, peeled and cut
  into fine slivers

Put the yoghurt in a bowl. Beat lightly with a whisk or a fork until smooth and creamy. Add the salt, pepper, cayenne, sugar, ginger and apple. Stir to mix.

Pour the oil into a small frying pan and set over a medium–high heat. When hot, put in the cumin seeds. Let them sizzle for 10 seconds, then add the shallot. Stir and fry over a medium heat until the shallot just starts to brown at the edges. Empty the contents of the pan, including the oil, into the yoghurt mixture. Stir to mix.

Courgette Yoghurt

Here is a typical Gujarati dish: slightly sweet, slightly salty, slightly hot and dotted with mustard seeds. I just love it. In India it would be served with a meal, but if you are in the habit of having a yoghurt for lunch, try this very nutritious version   **Serves 4**

285 g/10 oz courgette, coarsely grated

350 ml/12 fl oz natural yoghurt

¾ teaspoon salt

1 teaspoon caster sugar

freshly ground black pepper

⅛ teaspoon cayenne pepper, or to taste

2 teaspoons olive or rapeseed oil

½ teaspoon whole brown or yellow mustard seeds

2 fresh bird's eye chillies, partially slit, or 3 long slivers cut from a jalapeño chilli

8 fresh curry leaves or 4 fresh basil leaves, torn

Put the courgette into a small pan along with 150 ml/5 fl oz water. Bring to the boil. Cover, lower the heat and simmer for 2 minutes. Empty into a sieve to drain, then refresh by letting cold water run over it. Squeeze out as much of the water as you can.

Put the yoghurt in a bowl. Add the salt, sugar, black pepper and cayenne pepper. Beat with a fork or whisk until smooth and creamy. Add the drained courgette and mix well.

Pour the oil into a small pan and set over a medium–high heat. When hot, put in the mustard seeds. As soon as they pop, a matter of seconds, add the chilli and curry leaves. Quickly take the pan off the heat and pour its contents over the yoghurt. Stir to mix.

Yoghurt Relish with Okra
This is a simple and delicious relish to serve at Indian meals **Serves 4**

2 tablespoons olive or rapeseed oil

¼ teaspoon whole brown or yellow mustard seeds

12 medium-sized okra, topped and tailed, then cut crossways into 7-mm/⅓-inch slices

salt

250 ml/8 fl oz natural yoghurt

⅛ teaspoon cayenne pepper, or to taste

Pour the oil into a small frying pan and set over a medium–high heat. When hot, put in the mustard seeds. As soon as they start to pop, a matter of seconds, put in the okra. Stir for 1 minute. Reduce the heat to medium–low. Stir and fry for 8–10 minutes, or until the okra is lightly browned. Sprinkle ⅛ teaspoon salt over the okra, mix and take the pan off the heat. Set aside.

Put the yoghurt in a bowl. Whisk lightly with a fork until creamy. Add ¼ teaspoon salt and the cayenne pepper. Stir to mix.

Just before eating, fold the entire contents of the frying pan into the yoghurt.

Yoghurt Relish with Spinach

Any soft green, such as Swiss chard leaves, may be used instead of spinach in this recipe **Serves 4**

2 tablespoons olive or rapeseed oil

¼ teaspoon whole brown or yellow mustard seeds

½ clove garlic, peeled and sliced

140–180 g/5–6 oz fresh spinach leaves, chopped

salt

250 ml/8 fl oz natural yoghurt

⅛ teaspoon cayenne pepper, or to taste

Pour the oil into a small frying pan and set over a medium–high heat. When hot, put in the mustard seeds. As soon as they start to pop, a matter of seconds, put in the garlic. Stir for a few seconds. Add the spinach and stir for about 5 minutes, or until it is just cooked through. Add about ¼ teaspoon salt and mix it in.

Put the yoghurt in a bowl. Whisk lightly with a fork until creamy. Add ¼ teaspoon salt and the cayenne pepper. Stir to mix.

Just before eating, fold the entire contents of the frying pan into the yoghurt.

Yoghurt with Tomatoes & Chickpeas

Here is an easy, everyday yoghurt relish. I like to use a good full-fat yoghurt, but if you prefer a low-fat variety, it would work well too. My cherry tomatoes were on the large side, so I cut each into eight pieces. If yours are smaller, use more than suggested and just quarter them. Serve this relish with most Indian meals, or eat by itself as a snack **Serves 3–4**

300 ml/10 fl oz natural yoghurt

¼ teaspoon salt, or to taste

freshly ground black pepper

1 tablespoon peeled and very finely chopped red onion or shallot

155 g/5½ oz drained, cooked chickpeas (organic if canned)

about 3 large cherry tomatoes, cut into 8 pieces each

1 tablespoon chopped fresh coriander

a small pinch of cayenne pepper

Put the yoghurt in a bowl. Beat lightly with a whisk or fork until smooth. Add all the other ingredients. Stir to mix. Taste and adjust the seasonings as needed.

Sri Lankan Mustard Paste

Here is a condiment that I just cannot live without. You can add a dollop to curries or use it as you might any prepared mustard. It perks up hotdogs, my husband smears it on bacon and ham, it goes with roast beef, and is a lovely, pungent addition to sandwiches. We always keep a jar in the refrigerator. Try smearing it on fresh pineapple slices to serve with a curry meal, or on a ham or pork roast (see recipe below), or use it to make a vegetable pickle (see page 253.) **Makes a 250-ml/8-fl oz jar**

6 tablespoons whole brown or yellow mustard seeds

3 large cloves garlic, peeled and finely chopped

1 x 4-cm/1½-inch piece of fresh ginger, peeled and finely chopped

250 ml/8 fl oz cider vinegar or red wine vinegar, plus a little more, as needed

3 teaspoons cayenne pepper

3½ teaspoons salt

¼ teaspoon ground turmeric

4 teaspoons caster sugar

Combine the mustard seeds, garlic, ginger and vinegar in a bowl. Cover and leave overnight.

Empty the contents of the bowl into a blender and blend until you have a paste. If the blender is sluggish or the paste too thick, add another 2–3 teaspoons of vinegar. The density of the paste should be that of Dijon mustard.

Add the cayenne, salt, turmeric and sugar. Whizz once to mix, then taste for balance of seasonings. Put in a sterilised jar and leave to mellow, unrefrigerated, for 3 days. After that time the paste may be refrigerated and used as it is, or to make pickles and relishes. It lasts for at least a year in the refrigerator.

Pineapple Relish with Mustard Paste

Nose-tingling and refreshing, this Sri Lankan relish goes well with all curry meals. You could also serve it at Western meals with roast pork or pork chops **Serves 6**

about 560 g/1¼ lb peeled and diced fresh pineapple

3 tablespoons Sri Lankan Mustard Paste (see above)

Put the pineapple in a bowl. Add the paste and stir to mix. It will last for 2–3 days in the refrigerator.

Vegetable Pickle with Sri Lankan Mustard Paste

(*Singhala Achcharu*) When I first ate this Sri Lankan pickle, it was made with green beans and carrots, but it can be made with other vegetables as well, including cauliflower and green papaya, the latter found in Thai and South Asian grocers. You may combine all these vegetables if you like, cutting each of them so that the pieces are more or less of the same size **Makes 2 x 400-g/14-oz jars**

2 tablespoons salt

180 g/6 oz green beans, trimmed and cut crossways into 2-cm/¾-inch pieces

3 medium carrots, peeled and cut into the same size pieces as the beans

1 quantity Sri Lankan Mustard Paste (see page 252)

Pour 2 litres/70 fl oz water into a large pan and bring to a rolling boil. Add the salt and green beans. Boil for 30 seconds, then add the carrots. Boil for 30 seconds, then quickly drain. Shake out all the water and put the vegetables in a bowl. Add the mustard paste and mix.

Put the vegetables in a sterilised jar and leave to mature in the refrigerator for 3 days. It will last for a good year if kept refrigerated.

Easy Masala Chai (Spiced Tea)

At India's roadside tea stalls *masala chai* is served already sweetened. I have added about one teaspoon of sugar per cup in this recipe, which makes the tea just mildly sweet. You may double that amount if you prefer **Serves 4**

1/16 teaspoon ground cinnamon

1/16 teaspoon ground cloves

1/16 teaspoon ground cardamom (if you do not have it, throw in 4 whole cardamom pods)

1/16 teaspoon ground ginger

freshly ground black pepper

3 teabags containing good, unflavoured black tea (I use PG Tips)

500 ml/16 fl oz full-fat milk

4 teaspoons sugar

Put 750 ml/24 fl oz cold water in a pan. Add the ground spices, 4–5 generous grinds of black pepper and the teabags. Bring to the boil. Cover, reduce the heat to very, very low and simmer gently for 10 minutes.

Add the milk and sugar. Stir and bring to a simmer. Remove from the heat, pour through a fine sieve and serve.

Sweet Yoghurt Lassi

Originally a Punjabi word, lassi, the name of a yoghurt drink, has now been adopted by much of northern India and the world. It can be made from yoghurt thinned with water or with milk, as they do in the Punjab, where they like their drink tall and rich, or from 'traditional' (Indian) buttermilk, which is what is left when thinned-out yoghurt or milk is churned and the butter is removed. In India lassis may be consumed at breakfast or lunch, or as a daytime snack. In the north they tend to be quite simple: salty or sweet. The salty ones are seasoned with salt and perhaps some ground roasted cumin, while the sweet ones have sugar added, and perhaps some cardamom. In the south the yoghurt drinks tend to include mustard seeds, curry leaves, red chillies, ginger and even fresh coriander. These are often poured over rice, though they may be drunk as well **Serves 1 as a long drink; 2–3 as a small drink**

250 ml/8 fl oz natural yoghurt, preferably Greek or 'bio'

1 tablespoon caster sugar

4 cardamom pods

Combine all the ingredients plus 120 ml/4 fl oz cold water in a blender. Blend for 2 minutes. Strain and serve as is, or with a couple of ice cubes if desired.

Sweet Mango Lassi

These days all manner of inventive lassis are served everywhere, with all kinds of fruit and seasoning in them, from mangoes to bananas and guavas. Feel free to improvise. You can use full-fat yoghurt (I like Greek or 'bio' yoghurts best) or low-fat yoghurt – whatever you prefer. This recipe is best made when good fresh mangoes are in season. When they are not, very good-quality canned pulp made from India's excellent Alphonso mangoes can be used instead. Most Indian grocers sell this **Serves 2**

250 ml/8 fl oz natural yoghurt, preferably Greek or 'bio'

fresh ripe mangoes, peeled and chopped (enough to yield 250 ml/8 fl oz of pulp)

4 cardamom pods

2 tablespoons caster sugar

Put all the ingredients plus 120 ml/4 fl oz cold water into a blender and blend for 2 minutes. Taste for sweetness, adding more sugar if necessary.

Strain and serve as it is, or with a couple of ice cubes if desired.

Spices, Seasonings, Oils & Techniques

In order to make the recipes in this book easier to prepare, I have used a somewhat limited palette of spices and seasonings. Nonetheless, a fair number of them are still required. Most can be bought from Indian grocers or via the internet. Store the dried spices, preferably in their whole form, in tightly closed containers in a closed cupboard, away from sunlight. For optimum flavour, grind them as needed in a mortar or specially reserved coffee-grinder. The ones you use most could be stored in a spice box, as sold by Indian grocers – a round, stainless-steel box with stainless-steel containers inside it.

I suggest you start by getting only the spices you need for the specific dishes you wish to cook. Add more spices as you need them – don't overwhelm yourself.

This section also includes some techniques, such as how to grate tomatoes and ginger. Just look under the ingredient names, which are arranged alphabetically.

Asafoetida
This is one of the seasonings that I consider essential as it goes to the heart of Indian cooking. It is a resin, and not much is needed in a recipe. Only a very small amount gives many Indian dishes their earthy, truffle-like flavour and aroma. It is also a digestive and therefore used frequently with dals. Buy the ground version in the smallest size available and keep the container tightly closed.

Ata *See* Chapati Flour.

Black pepper
Native to India, whole black peppercorns are added to rice and meat dishes for a mild peppery-lemony flavour. Ground pepper was once used in large amounts, sometimes several tablespoons in a single dish, especially in south India, where it grows. The arrival of chillies from the New World around AD 1498 has changed that usage somewhat, though it still exists. In some south Indian dishes peppercorns are lightly roasted before use to draw out their lemony taste. In rice and meat dishes they are often used whole. Indians always leave them on the side, just as you would meat bones or a bay leaf. There's no need to get the most expensive kind; you would simply be paying for size and evenness of shape, which hardly matter.

Cardamom pods & seeds
Small green pods, the fruit of a ginger-like plant, hold clusters of black, highly aromatic seeds smelling like a combination of camphor, eucalyptus, orange peel and lemon. Whole pods are put into rice and meat dishes, while ground seeds are the main flavour in garam masala (see page 264). This versatile spice is the vanilla of India, and used in most desserts and sweetmeats. It is also added to spiced tea and sucked as a mouth freshener. Cardamom seeds that have been taken out of their pods are

sold separately by Indian grocers. If you cannot get them, take the seeds out of the pods yourself. The most aromatic pods are green in colour. White ones sold by supermarkets have been bleached and have less flavour.

When whole cardamom pods are put into dishes, they are not meant to be eaten. As with other large spices, such as cinnamon and bay leaves, they are left on the side of the plate, just as meat bones would be.

Cayenne Pepper *See* Chillies.

Chaat masala
A spice mixture containing sour mango powder, roasted cumin, cayenne pepper and other seasonings. It adds a spicy sourness. All Indian grocers sell this.

Chapati flour
Very finely ground wholemeal flour used to make chapatis, pooris and other Indian flatbreads. Sometimes called *ata*, it is sold by all Indian grocers and some supermarkets. An equal mixture of wholemeal and plain flour may be substituted.

Chicken stock
Many of my recipes call for chicken stock. These days you can buy it canned or freshly made from good grocers and butchers. I tend to collect leftover chicken and bones in my freezer, and when I have enough I put it all in a pot along with a peeled carrot and a peeled onion, a bay leaf, a little salt and enough cold water to cover everything by about 2.5 cm/1 inch. I bring this to the boil, skim it, and then let the pot simmer very gently for 2 hours. I strain this stock and put it in the refrigerator. The next day I remove the congealed fat, and the stock is ready to use.

Chillies
While Mexico uses dozens of varieties of chilli in its cuisine, India, which was gifted this new spice in the early 15th century, uses mostly the cayenne type, though they are rarely as fiery as the cayenne chillies I grow in my American backyard. Indian chillies are very thin-skinned, and usually 4–7.5 cm/1½–3 inches long. Indian grocery shops sell both the fresh and dried types of the chillies that are required for my recipes. Chinese grocers also sell the dried ones, as they are the same as those used in Sichuan food.

Fresh, hot green chillies
Many of the dishes in this book call for fresh, hot, green chillies. What should you use? Indian grocers sell a long cayenne-type chilli and the small, thin bird's eye chilli. Both are fine to use for Indian food. But what if you are not near an Indian shop? You can get fresh bird's eye chillies from Thai grocers. Failing that, you could use the much larger, thicker-skinned jalapeños

and serranos chillies, which are very different but may be used in their fresh form with this proviso: check if they are hot by cutting one in half lengthways, and then cutting off a sliver of skin to taste. If it is not hot, it won't serve any purpose at all. If it is hot, look at the recipe. If it calls for 1 chilli, use about a quarter of the jalapeño or about half of the serrano, cut lengthways, *with seeds*. Because of the thick skin, it is best to chop up the chilli finely, or use slivers if the recipe suggests whole chillies.

It is not always possible to gauge the heat of green chillies correctly. It is best to start with the smaller amount suggested in the recipe and then add more a little later in the cooking process, should you desire it.

Dried, hot red chillies When my recipes call for these, look for exactly the same chilli that is used in Sichuan cookery – red, about 5 cm/2 inches long and 7 mm/⅓ inch wide. These are often dropped into very hot oil. This process fries the skin and flavours the oil, giving whatever is cooked in it a special browned chilli taste.

Chilli powder, cayenne pepper Indians use pure chilli powder, unmixed with any other spices. Cayenne pepper is a fine substitute. They also use Kashmiri chillies, either powdered or whole, for a very special reason – they impart a lovely red colour to all foods and are not very hot. These special chillies grow in Kashmir and are similar to

the chillies used in making paprika. They are almost impossible to get in their whole form in the West, though some shops do sell a ground version that I do not entirely trust because it looks unnaturally red. For dishes where I might have used ground Kashmiri chillies, I substitute a combination of cayenne pepper mixed with paprika.

Chickpea flour Also sold as *gram* flour or *besan*. Almost no South Asian home is without chickpea flour. It is used to make fritters, dumplings and a whole family of snack foods. It is also used to thicken soupy stews, and added to yoghurt sauces when they are being heated to prevent curdling.

Cinnamon Used mainly for desserts in the West, cinnamon, often in its stick form, is added to many Indian meat and rice dishes for its warm, sweet aroma. Sri Lankans use it even more as it is one of their cash crops. This inner bark from a laurel-like tree is also an important ingredient in the aromatic mixture garam masala (see page 264).

Cloves Western cooks call for cloves when making desserts. Indians rarely use cloves in desserts, but do use them in rice, legume and meat dishes, and in the spice mixture garam masala (see page 264). Indians carry the pungently aromatic cloves, as well as cardamom pods, in tiny silver boxes and use them as mouth-fresheners. For the same reason, cloves are always part of the betel leaf paraphernalia that is offered as a digestive at the end of Indian meals.

Coconut Some of my recipes call for freshly grated coconut. This is now sold in frozen form at many Asian and Thai grocers. Look for the more finely grated kind: you should not be able to see coarse strands. Hack off what you need and keep the rest frozen.

You may also use unsweetened desiccated coconut. Just barely cover it with hot water and leave for 1 hour. Two tablespoons of desiccated coconut will yield about 3 tablespoons of a rough equivalent to grated fresh coconut.

Coconut milk I use the canned variety. Choose a brand you like and shake well. What is not used may either be stored in the refrigerator for a week, or frozen.

Coriander, fresh This is the parsley of southern Asia. Wash well and use just the leaves and more delicate stems. To store, stick the fresh coriander bunch in a glass of water like cut flowers and drape a plastic bag over the greenery.

Coriander seeds, whole & ground
Coriander seeds are best bought whole and then ground in small quantities as needed. This can be done in a clean coffee-grinder

or mortar. The crushing is very easy in a mortar: I do it all the time and the aroma is glorious.

Cumin seeds, whole & ground
The whole seeds look like caraway, only plumper and lighter in colour. You can buy them in their ground form, or grind them yourself in an electric grinder or clean coffee-grinder. Unlike ground coriander, the flavour of cumin lasts a long time.

To make roasted ground cumin seeds
Put a few tablespoons of seeds in a small, cast-iron frying pan over a medium–high heat. Stir and roast for a few minutes, until the seeds are just a shade darker and give off a strong roasted aroma. Remove from the pan and allow to cool a bit, then grind in a clean coffee-grinder or crush in a mortar. Save what you do not use in a tightly lidded jar. It can be kept for several months.

Curry leaves These have an exotic, sunny, lemony aroma – that is why they are used. Only fresh leaves will do, as the dried ones have no flavour or aroma at all. Find a local source if you can, or use an internet one. Alternatively, try growing a curry plant (*Murraya koenigii*) in a sunny spot. Sometimes fresh basil makes an interesting substitute, but it does not work every time.

Curry powder Generally, curry powders contain a blend of spices, including cumin, coriander, turmeric, chilli powder, fenugreek and many more. The flavours and potency can vary. Sometimes I like to add a little curry powder to a soup or curry, along with other spices. The one I use is made by Bolst's, and I get the hot version.

Dal   In India dried beans, split peas and other legumes are all sold under the common name 'dal'. I have decided to use this name throughout the book as it is all- encompassing. Almost every dal comes in a whole form with skin and without skin, and in a split form with and without skin. Sometimes split peas, in very small amounts, can also be used as a seasoning. Urad dal, from a pea native to India, is often used that way in south Indian cooking, always in its pale, split and hulled form. It provides a nutty flavour. Other split peas, such as yellow split peas, may be substituted. Whole urad dal, with its dark skin, is much loved in the Punjab, where it is known as whole *ma*.

Fennel seeds   These have an anise flavour and are wonderful with fish and vegetables such as aubergines.

Fenugreek seeds   Dull yellow and squarish, fenugreek seeds provide the earthy, musky taste in curry powders. They have a strong, lingering aroma and are frequently added to Indian pickles.

Garam masala   Literally 'warming spice mix', garam masala is a mixture of aromatic (and generally expensive) spices that, according to the ancient Ayurvedic system of medicine, are meant to heat the body. This is the only spice mixture that I ask you to make at home because it is so superior to what is sold in shops. Its aroma is unsurpassed if mixed and ground at home in small quantities. Also, it will not contain cheap 'filler' spices, such as coriander seeds, that you find in many commercial mixtures. However, I *do* keep the shop-bought mixture in my cupboard as well for use in certain dishes that require less perfume. My recipes will tell you which one to use.

Home-made garam masala

1 tablespoon cardamom seeds (shop-bought, or removed from pods yourself)
1 teaspoon whole cloves
1 teaspoon black peppercorns
1 teaspoon cumin seeds
⅓ of a nutmeg (hit it with a meat mallet or hammer to break it)
1 x 7.5-cm/3-inch cinnamon stick, broken up

Grind all these ingredients in a clean coffee-grinder and store in a dark cupboard.

Garlic   When crushed garlic is required I use a garlic press to get the pulp. It is quick and easy. You can also crush garlic by placing the flat side of a knife on it and hitting it with your fist.

Ghee This is clarified butter, made by boiling down a large quantity of butter until all the water in it evaporates and the milk solids turn hard. It is then strained and ready to be used for all kinds of cooking, including deep-frying. Ghee can be bought from Indian grocers, but you might find that it is made in the Netherlands!

Ginger I have used mainly fresh ginger in this book. This rhizome has a sharp, pungent, cleansing taste and is a digestive to boot. It is now said to help with travel sickness as well. Ginger should be stored in a dry, cool place. Many people like to bury it in dryish, sandy soil. This way they can break off and retrieve small portions as they need them, while the rest of the knob generously keeps growing.

To prepare finely grated ginger
When a recipe requires, say, a 2.5-cm/1-inch piece of fresh ginger to be grated, it is best to keep that piece attached to the large knob. The knob acts as a handle and saves you from grating your fingers. Peel just the part you require, then grate it on the finest part of a grater (preferably a ginger grater or fine Microplane grater) so that it turns into pulp.

To cut slices of ginger Peel a section of the knob and cut crossways into thinnish slices.

To cut slivers of ginger Cut the ginger into very thin slices (as described above), then stack them 6 or 7 slices at a time and cut into very fine strips (slivers).

To cut ginger into minute dice Cut slivers of ginger (as described above), then cut them crossways into very fine dice.

Gram flour *See* Chickpea flour

Kaffir lime leaves These highly aromatic, lemony green leaves are sold by Thai grocers. They look like two leaves joined together, top to bottom. The skin of the lime itself is also used in Thai cookery. I was not aware that they were used in South Asian cookery until I went to Bangladesh and smelt that distinct aroma in a dal. What leaves you do not use can be frozen. I actually went to New York's China Town and bought myself a plant. It is now happily producing limes as well.

Lemon grass There are just a few recipes in this book where I have used lemon grass. It provides a lemony aroma to Sri Lankan stews and rice dishes. As the grass stalks are tall and hard, you need to cut off and discard the top, leaving about 15 cm/6 inches of the bottom. You must then hit the bulbous bottom end with a hammer to crush it lightly. Now the stalk is ready to go into a pot of stew or a rice dish.

Mustard seeds
India has mustard seeds of several colours – pale yellow, black and brown. The brown are indigenous and most widely used. All mustard seeds have two distinct characteristics: if they are thrown into very hot oil, they pop and develop a nutty flavour; if they are ground, they become pungent and slightly bitter. In south Asia they are used in both forms. As they roll around easily, I grind them in a clean coffee-grinder. If you cannot find brown seeds, substitute the yellow variety.

Nigella (*Kalonji*)
You might have seen these black, tear-shaped seeds on top of Indian flatbreads, such as naans. I love their oregano-like aroma. They are used in Bengal and through much of northern India for pickling, for flavouring vegetables, such as aubergines, and for fish curries.

Nutmeg
The seed of a round, pear-like fruit, the slightly camphorous nutmeg is used in the making of the aromatic spice mixture known as garam masala (see page 264). To break the nut into smaller pieces, just tap it lightly with a hammer or meat mallet.

Oils
I have used ordinary olive oil (not extra virgin) and rapeseed oil in this book just to keep the choices manageable, but you could use corn or peanut oil just as easily. For special dishes from Bengal or Kashmir, I use mustard oil, which is available from Indian grocers.

Onions
There are two kinds of onion commonly used in India – the shallot in most of the south and Sri Lanka, and a smallish, pink onion in the north. Indeed, in northern India the word for our onion is *pyaz*, and the pink colour is *pyazi*. A medium onion weighs about 140 g/5 oz.

Paprika
Kashmir, India's northernmost state, produces a chilli powder that is rather like paprika. It is mild and imparts a lovely red colour. To get the same effect, I often combine cayenne pepper with sweet paprika, making sure that the paprika is fresh and still has a good red colour. Old paprika that has been sitting around turns brownish and is of no use for the recipes in this book.

Poppadoms
These fine wafers are generally made from a split-pea dough and dried in the sun. Indian grocers sell them plain or studded with black pepper or cumin seeds, or green or red chillies, or garlic – the choices are many. When buying poppadoms, make sure they are pliable and therefore fresh. Keep them well sealed. To serve, they can be deep-fried for a few seconds in hot oil, roasted over a fire, toasted under a grill,

or cooked in a microwave oven on full power for 40–50 seconds.

Saffron Only 'leaf' saffron (whole saffron threads) is used in this book. Known in ancient Greece and Rome, as well as in ancient Persia and India, this valued spice consists of the whole dried stigma of a special autumn crocus. Look for a reliable source of saffron as it is very expensive and there can be a great deal of adulteration. Indians often roast the saffron threads lightly in a cast-iron frying pan before soaking them in a tablespoon or two of hot milk to bring out the colour. This milk is then poured over rice to give it orange highlights. In Iran the saffron is crushed with a cube of sugar and allowed to soak in a mixture of melted butter before it is used. This also brings out its colour. In much of European cookery a very light pinch of saffron is thrown directly into stock to make risottos and soups.

Squash We are beginning to find peeled and seeded butternut squash in our supermarkets now but those who cannot find it will need to use a peeler to get the skin off. The ease or difficulty of preparing squash depends on the thickness of the skin. If it's too thick to remove with a vegetable peeler, try the following steps:

How to peel butternut squash Place the squash on a board. Using a very sharp knife, cut off and discard the stem end. Cut off the neck at the point where it begins to flare out. Stand the neck on the board and use a sharp knife to remove the skin by slicing downwards all the way around. Peel the bulbous base of the squash in the same way. Halve or quarter the peeled pieces lengthways. Using a spoon, scrape out the seeds and fibres. Cut the flesh into whatever size pieces you need.

Tomatoes My recipes often call for grated tomatoes. This is the quickest way to get a rough tomato sauce. Grating them does include the seeds, but I have never understood why we throw them away. However, it does get rid of the skin, which can be unsightly in a sauce. I have never seen tomatoes grated anywhere except in India. Here is how you go about it:

How to grate tomato Use the coarsest side of a grater, like the one you find on a four-sided grater. When you start grating, the tomato may refuse to oblige and slip around. Press hard, or even cut off a thin slice on that side, and keep going. When you get to the end, flatten your palm and grate off as much as possible until only the skin is left. Discard the skin. A medium tomato weighs about 140 g/5 oz and yields about 120 ml/4 fl oz fresh sauce.

To peel tomatoes Provided the tomatoes are firm, the quickest and easiest way to peel them is by using a vegetable peeler or paring knife.

To make tomato passata Wash the tomatoes and let them dry. Chop coarsely, removing the sepals and stems, and put them into a pan that holds them easily. Crush the tomato pieces first with your hands to release their juices, then turn the heat on medium–low and let them come to a simmer slowly. The low heat allows more juices to ooze out slowly. Add just a tiny bit of salt as this helps release the juices. Once the tomatoes are bubbling, turn the heat up to medium and let the sauce bubble away, simmering vigorously until it is thick. Stir now and then so that it doesn't catch. Let the passata cool, then push it through a coarse sieve or place in a blender. Pour the passata into small plastic bags or jars (120–150 ml/4–5 fl oz), then seal and freeze.

Turmeric A rhizome like ginger, only with smaller, more delicate 'fingers', fresh turmeric is quite orange inside. When dried, it turns bright yellow. It is the musky yellow powder produced from this that gives some Indian dishes a yellowish cast. As it is cheap and is also considered to be an antiseptic, it is used freely in the cooking of legumes and vegetables. Its colour can stain, so use with care.

Index